WEDGWOOD

WEDGWOOD

Geoffrey Wills

CHARTWELL
BOOKS, INC.

Above: *A selection of jasper ware*　　　***Overleaf:*** *Blue and white jasper girandole*

First published in Britain 1980 by
Country Life Books and distributed by the
Hamlyn Publishing Group Ltd

This 1989 edition published by
CHARTWELL BOOKS, INC.,
A Division of BOOK SALES, INC.,
110 Enterprise Avenue,
Secaucus, New Jersey 07094

ISBN 1 55521 389 8

Produced by Mandarin Offset
Printed and bound in Hong Kong

CONTENTS

FOREWORD

All who write on Wedgwood owe a big debt to Eliza Meteyard. It was she who penned the first important book on the subject; a book that is still indispensable after more than one hundred years.

Joseph Mayer, who was born at Newcastle-under-Lyme but made his home and his fortune at Liverpool, allowed Miss Meteyard full access to his great hoard of Wedgwood documents. These he had found in 1848 under what might be considered unpropitious circumstances: caught in a sudden downpour when in a Birmingham suburb, he took shelter in a rag-shop where he had the incredible luck to discover the majority of the Wedgwood records that had been disposed of following the death of Josiah II in 1843. In the intervening five years, much of the accumulation had been sold to local shopkeepers as wrapping-paper. In due course the papers rescued by Mayer came into the possession of Josiah Wedgwood & Sons who, in turn, have deposited them at the University of Keele.

In addition to being grateful for the pioneering work of Eliza Meteyard, the present writer acknowledges with thanks various forms of assistance rendered by the undermentioned:

the many who have contributed to the pages of the **Proceedings** *of the Wedgwood Society; Alison Kelly, Editor of the* **Proceedings**, *for the loan and use of the manuscript of her article on the Catherine service; J.K. des Fontaines, Chairman of the Wedgwood Society, for kindly allowing use of his researches into Wedgwood bone china; H.L. Douch, Curator of the County Museum, Truro, for drawing attention to an advertisement in the* **Sherborne Mercury**; *and for unstinted aid, Gaye Blake-Roberts and Lynn Miller, respectively Curator and Information Officer at the Wedgwood Museum, Barlaston; and Derek Halfpenny, Public Relations Director of Josiah Wedgwood & Sons.*

Left: *Jasper plaque of 'Diomedes gazing at the Palladium', circa 1775. Wedgwood Museum, Barlaston*

Staffordshire teapot and cover, circa 1750, of unglazed red stoneware,
introduced in the 1690s by the Elers brothers, with impressed imitation Chinese seal

Chapter One

EARLY DAYS

Josiah Wedgwood was born in 1730 in Burslem, Staffordshire, an area well known for its established and varied pottery tradition. He was apprenticed at the age of fourteen to his eldest brother, and some ten years later formed a partnership with a leading local potter, Thomas Whieldon. Trained to throw vessels on the potter's wheel from the beginning of his apprenticeship, but later prevented from practising by a knee injury, Josiah turned his talents to experimenting with different materials, shapes, techniques and finishes, thereby laying the foundations for the phenomenal success of the firm of Wedgwood.

The numerous individual potteries or 'pot-banks' were small concerns, almost all of them worked by their owner with the aid of a few employees, often including some relatives. It is necessary to discuss the earlier products and the methods of their manufacture in order to appreciate the advances due to the enterprise of Josiah Wedgwood.

The traditional goods of the district were for a long time of a coarse type, mostly made in a heavily glazed red clay and ornamented in a variety of ways that demanded limited skill. The composition of the glaze included a proportion of lead oxide and, unavoidably, impurities in the form of iron that gave it a yellow-brown cast. The majority of the objects made were dishes and pots of all sizes and shapes and, although some of them were intended as decoration in the home, most were severely functional.

Some new and better finished types of ware were introduced in the late 17th century, and these soon superseded the older and less sophisticated kind. In one instance, the red clay was employed after having been treated for the removal of impurities to make it of a fine texture, and then fired in a considerably hotter kiln than had been customary. This ware was first produced in Staffordshire by two brothers, John Philip and David Elers, who came from Holland and worked in the county for a few

In northern Staffordshire two materials led to the founding of an industry: an abundance of clay suitable for making pottery, and the coal to feed the kilns. This industry began by supplying local requirements, but by the outset of the 18th century was sending many of its products farther afield. In the course of time, the area became known as 'the Potteries'.

Above: *Miniature portrait of Josiah Wedgwood, thought to date from circa 1758, when Wedgwood was in his late twenties.*

years from 1693. The red pottery they made was finished without a glaze, the great heat of the kiln having vitrified the clay, making it watertight. The teapots and other objects attributed to these two men were either quite plain and smooth, or ornamented with relief patterns.

Redware

Another improvement has traditionally been attributed to a local potter, John Astbury, who died in 1743. He is said to have been the first to import and use white clay from Devonshire, with which he made contrasting reliefs on his redware. Astbury, like the Elers brothers, made his ornaments with metal stamps, moistening the dried clay object and sticking each relief in position. This simple method of 'sprigging' was improved by the use of moulds made of unglazed pottery or plaster,

Below: A beautiful Whieldon-type teapot and cover in the shape of a melon. Circa 1755–60

11

Above: Staffordshire redware teapot and cover. Contrasting white clay reliefs were made with metal stamps, then stuck to the dried red clay and glazed

which gave much better results. Soft clay was pressed into the mould, carefully removed and then affixed as before.

Some of Astbury's contemporaries made articles of red, locally found white, and stained clays semi-blended to form more-or-less realistic imitations of natural stones and marbles. These were known as 'agate' wares which, being of the same substance throughout, are to be distinguished from another variety named 'marbled', patterned only on the surface.

Salt-glazed stoneware

A further innovation in Staffordshire was salt-glazed stoneware, which had long been known in Germany but was first made in England by John Dwight of Fulham only in the third quarter of the 17th century. It was manufactured from white clay that had been rendered more manageable when plastic, and both more durable and white when fired, by the inclusion of powdered flints. The hard stones were calcined: that is, they were heated until red-hot, cooled, and ground to produce a fine white powder to be mixed with Devonshire or other clay before being fired at a high temperature. However, fragments excavated on the sites of Staffordshire potteries have shown that much of the ware was made from a coarse near-white clay mixed with sand. Before firing, the articles were each dipped in a locally dug pipeclay slip so that they were completely covered. The finished ware differed very little in appearance from that of clay and flint throughout, and the deception is usually only revealed by chipping or breakage. The use of cheaper ingredients found in the neighbourhood kept down the cost and the selling price of 'dipware', and it continued to be made for several decades.

Below: *Two Astbury-Whieldon ware coffee pots, circa 1755–60. The earthenware is lead-glazed, with applied decoration*

Above: *Worcester tankard, circa 1745. The skilful blue and white decoration is in the Chinoiserie style, which was immensely popular at this time*

The Germans discovered that a decorative glaze could be given to such ware by the use of common salt, which was shovelled into the kiln when the contents were at red heat.

A mixture of white clay, local or imported, together with flints, began to be used with a lead glaze, but fired at a similar temperature to that used for the red wares. This was done because the glaze could not withstand the heat required for stoneware, but had the advantage of being cheaper to make as it needed less fuel. In due course the lead-glazed pottery with its yellowish tint was gradually improved and became known as creamware. For a long time, the glaze was applied to the naturally dried clay article in the form of powdered galena (sulphide of lead) or lead oxide (litharge: white or red lead); a single firing completed the operation.

According to tradition, *c.* 1750 Enoch Booth of Tunstall discovered that a marked improvement resulted from the use of a liquid glaze. This was applied to the object after it had first been fired to an unglazed 'biscuit' state, when it was dipped in a liquefied mixture of ground lead and flints before a second firing.

One other ware deserves a mention: 'Black Egyptian' which was a black unglazed hard pottery, a stoneware, that was the same colour throughout. According to one writer it gained its name from its general resemblance to classical Greek and Roman black pottery, but may have been so-called because its colour recalled the dark skins and jet black hair of gypsies who were sometimes known in the past as 'Egyptians'. This ware was made either from clay containing manganese in its composition or from a dark red clay to which oxide of manganese was added. Jugs and teapots were, according to Simeon Shaw, the principal products of makers of this type of pottery.

The Staffordshire potworks were to be found in groups, having been established whenever suitable deposits of clay existed. In time, the hamlets expanded and were linked to one another by tracks and roads. The largest of the communities was at Burslem, 'the mother of the Potteries'.

Simeon Shaw stated that the Burslem district boasted about twenty-two kilns at the close of the 17th century, adding, 'no manufacturer of that period fired more than one oven full weekly, commencing on the Thursday night, and finishing about mid-day on Saturday'.

Above: *The Gladstone Potteries, Staffordshire. The potworks chimneys, belching forth smoke from the fierce heat of the kiln, were familiar landmarks in the Potteries district*

The Wedgwood family

The town shared its name with that of a family, one of whom, Margaret Burslem, in 1612 married Gilbert Wedgwood who had settled in the area. Other Wedgwoods, direct or indirect descendants of Gilbert, owned potteries in the neighbourhood of Burslem and elsewhere, the Churchyard pottery, Burslem, being from the mid-17th century owned by successive bearers of the name Thomas Wedgwood.

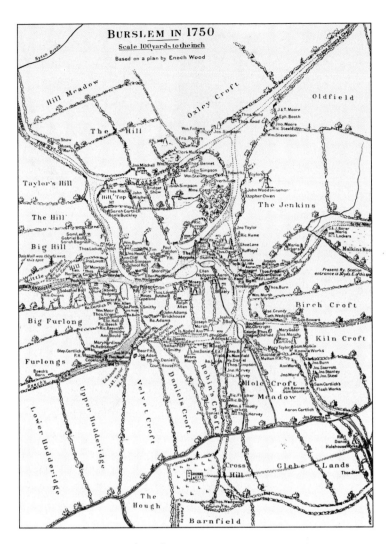

BURSLEM IN 1750
Scale 100 yards to the inch
Based on a plan by Enoch Wood

Above: Map dated 1750 of Burslem, known as 'the mother of the Potteries', and birthplace of Josiah Wedgwood in 1730

Thomas Wedgwood III, of the Churchyard, was born in 1687 and duly married Mary Stringer, daughter of a Unitarian minister of Newcastle-under-Lyme. According to John Ward, the historian of Stoke, their first child, Margaret, was followed over the years

by a dozen others: five girls and seven boys, the last being a boy they named Josiah. Other writers have stated that Josiah was the youngest of ten children, and others again have made him the youngest of twelve, Josiah C. Wedgwood, writing in 1908, subscribing to the last number. Similarly disputable is the exact date of his birth, but it is clearly recorded that he was baptised at Burslem on 12 July 1730. Notwithstanding these and other uncertainties regarding his early years, he was destined to transform the local pottery trade into an internationally recognised industry; one with which his own name, and that of his descendants, is inseparably linked.

Josiah's childhood

Considerable imagination has been exercised at various times in describing how the young Josiah may have spent his childhood, successive writers indulging in the maximum of deduction from the few recorded facts. There is no evidence to support the assertion of Llewellynn Jewitt that 'he was an amiable, thoughtful and particularly intelligent child, ever quiet and studious, and delighting more in thoughtful occupations than in the games and rough exercise of the boys of that, and indeed of every, time'. Eliza Meteyard suggested that he would have been a pupil at a dame-school in Burslem, 'more to be out of the way of mischief, than for the learning to be obtained there', although it is uncertain whether such an establishment existed in the place. When he was seven years of age it would appear

Above: *Portrait of the Wedgwood family painted by George Stubbs, famous for his paintings of animals, especially horses, during a visit to Etruria Hall in 1780*

that Josiah began to attend a school at Newcastle-under-Lyme, 'kept by a man of superior education named John or Thomas Blunt'. According to another tradition, the boy was adept at using a pair of scissors, apparently making what were later known as silhouettes of somewhat unusual subjects. These were said to have included

. . . an army at combat, a fleet at sea, a house and garden, or a whole pot-work, and the shapes of the ware made in it. These cuttings when wetted were stuck the whole length of the sloping desks, to the exquisite delight of the scholars . . .

One occurrence that must have affected Josiah's youth was the death of his father in 1739, when Thomas Wedgwood was 52 and his youngest child under nine years of age. The Churchyard pottery that had been inherited by Thomas was bequeathed by him to his eldest son, his namesake and the fourth of the family to become its owner. Each of the six younger children, who included Josiah, was to receive the sum of £20 on reaching the age of twenty, 'and that in paying the said sums, the elder shall be preferred before the younger'. The executors were charged with using any money 'not settled on my Wife' for the upbringing of the younger children. Their father's wishes, however, seem to have been ignored as it has been stated that Josiah immediately ceased to attend school and went to work under his brother at the Churchyard.

Whether he remained at school or not, it is known that he had the misfortune to contract smallpox when the disease made an appearance at Burslem, but the year in which this took place remains debatable. Some say 1741 and others 1746 or 1747. In any event, it would seem that the attack was a serious one, and after a period of convalescence Josiah found that his right knee remained so stiff as to seriously impede movement. The condition eased with time, but it was reported that he always required a walking stick.

Josiah's apprenticeship

The next certain fact is that on 11 November 1744 when he was fourteen years of age, Josiah was apprenticed to his eldest brother. The Indenture of apprenticeship made it clear that

. . . the said Josiah Wedgwood, of his own free Will and Consent, and with the Consent and Direction of his said Mother, Hath put and doth hereby Bind himselfe Apprentice unto the said Thomas Wedgwood, to Learn his Art, Mistery, Occupation, or Imployment of Throwing, and Handleing, which the said Thomas Wedgwood now useth . . .

He reputedly began his apprenticeship by learning how to throw, the art of making and shaping hollow vessels on the potter's wheel. The flat wheel, or circular board, was placed horizontally at a convenient working level, and an axle through its centre connected to another wheel at the base, this latter being made to revolve by the action of the worker's foot. There can be little doubt that the damage to his knee would have made it difficult for Wedgwood to operate the device, and it is assumed that he was forced to transfer his attention to other sides of the craft.

When his time with his brother terminated in 1752, Wedgwood entered into partnership with two men named John Harrison and Thomas Alders, at Cliff Bank, Stoke. Harrison was described by Jewitt as 'a man possessed of some means, but little taste', and he apparently provided capital for the venture. The output is said to have included stoneware articles, either plain or of the variety known as 'scratched blue'; the latter being decorated with patterns incised in the semi-soft clay which were dusted with blue for emphasis.

Many of the stoneware goods would

Above: Teapot in the style of Thomas Whieldon, circa 1760. Special features are the mottled 'tortoiseshell' glaze and oriental 'ling-lung' decoration

have been produced by press-moulding, or by the recently introduced process of slip-casting. In the former, a thin slab of soft clay was placed between two parts of a metal or alabaster mould, and then squeezed so as to receive the shape of the mould and the impression of any relief patterning in it. Slip-casting took advantage of the porous nature of plaster of Paris, of which patterned moulds were made. A quantity of liquefied clay, or 'slip' as it is called, was poured into the mould and after a few minutes was tipped out leaving a thin coating of clay within due to the absorption of water by the mould. The operation would be repeated until the layers formed a sufficient thickness and it was then allowed to dry and harden enough for the mould, which was made in close-fitting parts, to be removed. The undecorated surfaces of articles made by the foregoing methods vary and provide clues as to which was employed. Press-moulding leaves the area flat and smooth, while slip-casting results in the reverse side showing depressions where there are reliefs.

Partnership with Whieldon

By 1754 the Alders-Harrison-Wedgwood partnership broke up, and the latter entered into an agreement with one of the foremost potters of the period, Thomas Whieldon, of Fenton. Whieldon made a wide variety of goods, and from surviving documents it is clear that he was in business on what was then a large scale. Excavations carried out on the site of his principal pottery at Little Fenton, just to the north of Stoke-on-Trent, resulted in the discovery of quantities of fragments that included red clay wares, salt-glazed stoneware, and varieties of creamware. Many of the latter bore mottled glazes of the type known as 'tortoiseshell', because of a faint resemblance to that material, which has always been associated with Whieldon's name.

Articles of the above types were being made widely in Staffordshire by 1750, where there was an increasing awareness of competition from porcelain. This was more expensive to buy, whether imported from the mainland of Europe, the Far East or from one of the newly started English factories. Whatever its source, it set standards of quality in both appearance and durability that fully justified the cost for those who could afford it. Above all, its whiteness and attractive decoration had great appeal, which was especially merited in the case of plates and dishes where porcelain contrasted so favourably with the less appealing and less hygienic pewter and wood.

Among Josiah Wedgwood's fellow-workers at Thomas Whieldon's pottery was an apprentice, William Greatbatch, who became adept at devising new shapes and patterns. He worked as a designer for Whieldon, and when Wedgwood left in 1759 so did Greatbatch. It was Greatbatch who was responsible for designing the teapots and other articles in the form of fruit, made in creamware and coated in clear glazes, that are usually attributed to the years when Wedgwood and Whieldon were at Fenton. These pieces were the pottery-makers' attempt to compete with the comparable fashionable vegetable objects made in porcelain at nearby Longton Hall, and with the animals, birds and fishes, formed as tureens, produced at Chelsea.

When he was at Fenton, Wedgwood made many efforts to improve existing wares, and an unusual clause in his partnership agreement permitted him to keep to himself any discoveries he made: he was under no obligation to reveal them to his partner or to anyone else. It was at this time that he perfected a clear and bright green glaze that had been known in Tudor times and subsequently neglected.

Wedgwood's private notebook, in which are listed the above and other experiments, has survived, and is in the Wedgwood Museum at Barlaston. He prefaced it with an interesting survey of the output of the pottery at which he worked and a general picture of the state

Right: *Staffordshire coffee pot decorated in the form of a cauliflower. Circa 1755–1760*

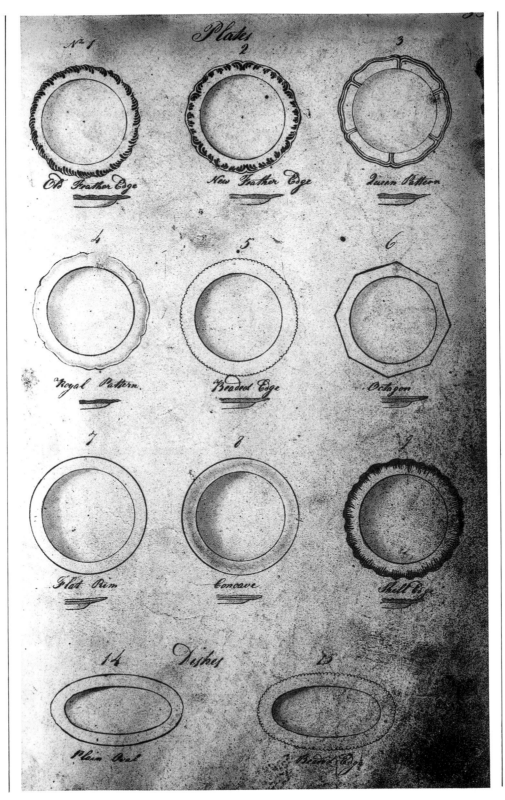

of the industry, drafted at the time and subsequently amplified:

This suite of experiments was begun at Fenton Hall, in the parish of Stoke upon Trent, about the beginning of the year 1759, in my partnership with Mr.Whieldon, for the improvement of our manufacture of earthenware, which at that time stood in great need of it, the demand for our goods decreasing daily, and the trade universally complained of as being bad & in a declining condition.

White Stone ware (viz. with Salt glaze) was the principal article of our manufacture. But this had been made a long time, and the prices were now reduced so low that the patters could not afford to bestow much expense upon it, or make it so good in any respect as the ware would otherwise admit of. And with regard to Elegance of form, that was an object very little attended to.

The next article in consequence to the Stoneware was an imitation of Tortoiseshell. But as no improvement has been made in this branch for several years, the country was grown weary of it; and though the price had been lowered from time to time, in order to increase the sale, the expedient did not answer, and something new was wanted, to give a little spirit to the business.

*I had already made an imitation of Agate; which was esteemed beautiful & a considerable improvement; but people were surfeited with wares of these variegated colours. These considerations induced me to try for some more solid improvements as well in the **Body**, as the **Glazes**, the **Colours**, & the **Forms**, of the articles of our manufacture.*

I saw the field was spacious, and the soil so good, as to promise an ample recompense to any one who should labour diligently in its cultivation.

Opposite: *Page of drawings from Wedgwood's 1802 Drawing Book, showing various designs for plates produced from the 1760s*

Below: *Josiah Wedgwood's distinctive autograph*

The final paragraph of Wedgwood's remarks was prophetic.

Left: *Staffordshire teapot in the shape of a pineapple;*
Centre: *Leeds punchpot;* **Right:** *Astbury-Whieldon teapot*

24

Chapter Two

THE BELL WORKS

Josiah Wedgwood began business on his own account at the Ivy House pot-bank in Burslem, later moving to the Brick House, which became known as the Bell Works. Here he developed his own brand of creamware, with some particularly fine fruit and vegetable pieces. He was to take full advantage of transfer-printing, a cheaper alternative to hand-painting, which gave sophisticated results in a variety of colours, and engine-turning, which gave pottery wares an attractive, distinctive finish. Soon, a London showroom had been established, and Wedgwood was commissioned to produce wares under royal patronage.

Following the termination of his partnership with Whieldon at Fenton, Josiah Wedgwood returned to his birthplace. Earlier, he had made plans to set up in business on his own account, for there survives an agreement he made with his cousin, Thomas Wedgwood. The document is dated at Stoke, 30 December, 1758, and by its terms Thomas 'engageth to serve the s^d. Josiah Wedgwood as a Journeyman from the first of May 1759'. There is some argument about the precise location of his first premises, Jewitt stating that he began by occupying the family's Churchyard pottery, but although he may have been elsewhere briefly at first it is agreed that he leased the Ivy House pot-bank. The owners were again relatives, John and Thomas Wedgwood,

Above: Engraving of the 'Ivy House' Works at Burslem, rented by Josiah Wedgwood from relatives, circa 1759

and for the kilns with the adjoining creeper-clad house in the centre of Burslem they charged him £10 a year.

The Bell Works

Within a couple of years Wedgwood had outgrown the Ivy House and took the lease of another Burslem pottery: the Brick House. It later became known as the Bell Works, because Josiah built on it a cupola in which hung a bell. With this his employees were summoned to work each day, an early example of Wedgwood's flair for publicity, and his continual careful regard for details.

Above: The Brick House, later Bell Works, Burslem, rented by Wedgwood circa 1763 to the early 1770s

He must have been aware instinctively that the fragmented Staffordshire industry could not compete much longer with cheaper and better imported goods, either pottery or porcelain. Despite the imposition of import duties, the public's appetite for them was seemingly insatiable and they continued to enter the country in large quantities. Porcelain, especially, was coming from China in an unending flood. It is not unlikely that Wedgwood knew of the letters explaining the details of porcelain-making sent back from the Far East by the French Jesuit missionary. Père d'Entrecolles. The letters had been printed in France soon after they were written, in 1712 and 1722, and again in a description of China by J.-B. du Halde that was first issued in Paris in 1735 and published in an English translation in 1738-41. D'Entrecolles described with great care the materials and processes in use at Ching-tê-Chên, where there were some 3,000 kilns and a population of one million employed in the industry in one capacity or another.

William Greatbatch

Soon after he became established on his own, Wedgwood was doing business with his old acquaintance, William Greatbatch. A note from the latter dated 22 July 1760 specifies a number of items 'Left at the Cross Keys, Wood

Street, London', an inn used by coaches with destinations as far apart as Hertford, Hoddesdon and Ware to the north of the city, Wantage to the west, and Norwich to the north-east. The goods included 'foxglove teapots', 'melon sauce boats and stands', and 'Woodbine' and 'Chinese' teapots. Examples of some of these and of the other patterns listed have been identified in stoneware and creamware.

The range of pieces formed as fruits, mentioned earlier as having been made in the Whieldon-Wedgwood era, included pineapples and vegetables, which were similarly glazed.

There is evidence in correspondence that Greatbatch was making blocks for Wedgwood as well as supplying him

with teapots and other items. Most, if not all, were unglazed and were given their finish by Wedgwood, and while some were of fine creamware throughout others were of a coarse clay that was disguised by the glaze. All are notable for clearcut modelling and their strong, pure colour.

Josiah was making his own creamware by 1761, if not a little earlier. Like that being made else-

Below: *Block mould for two teapot spouts and for a cauliflower teapot, all probably designed by William Greatbatch. Wedgwood Museum, Barlaston*

Above: Wedgwood-Whieldon teapot and cover in the form of a cauliflower. Wedgwood Museum, Barlaston

where, it was of a deep cream, almost buff, tone, and at first with a glaze that sometimes showed crazing: a network of fine cracks. It was to be some years before he was able to perfect a truly cream-colour earthenware with a near-colourless and even glaze.

The pottery trade

There is evidence that in the early 1760s Wedgwood was no less busy as a buyer and a salesman than a potter. Extant bills show that from 1762 he was engaged in buying pottery from several local makers; equally he was selling to them, but as none of the ware bore marks it is only possible to hazard a guess as to the source of surviving examples. How-ever, a feature pointing to a Wedgwood origin is to be found on his teapots; in many instances, Donald Towner gives the proportion among existing examples as being as high as 90 per cent. The spouts are of a distinctive pattern: they are moulded with over-lapping cabbage or cauliflower leaves, and used indis-criminately on plain or moulded pots, of the same design as the spouts of many of his vegetable and pineapple teapots. Saltglazed stoneware blocks of such spouts are to be seen in the Wedgwood Museum, Barlaston, having been discovered in 1905 at Etruria, where they had lain unnoticed for over a century.

To interest a wider public it was essential that the pottery should have a more sophisticated appearance. Moulded patterns in relief dimly seen through daubs of transparent coloured glazes were unlikely to prove of compelling interest to buyers who admired painted porcelain. Two other styles of ornamentation were available: straightforward painting, or the newly devised process of transfer printing. Small potteries did not always have resident decorators on their staffs, and in that case they could send the partly finished goods to specialist firms.

Painted wares

As regards painting, Wedgwood is known to have had an unspecified proportion of his ware decorated locally. He began to have dealings with David Rhodes of Leeds, perhaps the same Rhodes who later became his employee. In 1760 the *Leeds Intelligencer* carried an advertisement for Messrs Robinson and Rhodes, announcing that they enamelled all kinds of chinaware, and 'sell a good assortment of Foreign China and great variety of useful English China of the newest improvement, which they will engage to wear as well as Foreign, and will change gratis if broke with hot water'. A letter to Wedgwood signed by Rhodes 'for Partner and Self', dated 11 March 1763, contained an order for teapots and fruit baskets and dishes, adding 'we shall want many more of

them'. Without doubt these goods would have been undecorated and were painted as required by the recipients, who then sold them to their clients. There is no evidence at this date that Wedgwood was having his ware painted on his own account, and he was confining his own decorating to the application of coloured glazes in the Whieldon manner.

Pieces attributed to Robinson and Rhodes are painted in a naive and colourful manner with figures against rustic backgrounds, flowers, or with simple geometrical patterns, all of which would probably have had a greater appeal in the country than in London. There they would have been competing with the more skilfully decorated products of Chelsea, Bow, Worcester and other English porcelain factories as well as with imports.

Transfer printing

Josiah Wedgwood recognised that hand-painted work demanded skilled artists for its execution, and that such persons were difficult to find and expensive to employ. Printing as an acceptable alternative to painting became available very soon after he became established at Burslem, and Wedgwood soon took advantage of the opportunity it presented to reduce costs while maintaining quality.

Opposite: *Creamware teapot and cover, circa 1769, with characteristically colourful enamelling by David Rhodes*

Sadler and Green

Two Liverpool men, John Sadler and Guy Green, testified on oath in 1756 that they had successfully decorated 1,200 tiles with printed patterns in the space of six hours. They added in their statement that they had been 'upwards of seven years in finding out the method'. The process was equally applicable to enamels, pottery and porcelain.

Like so many other significant inventions, it was a surprisingly simple one: an engraving or woodcut was printed with special ink on thin paper, the image then being transferred to the glazed surface of the object to be decorated. Firing resulted in the design melting into the glaze and the finished article presented a smooth and shining appearance with the fine lines of the engraving clearly apparent. For Wedgwood's ware, black was commonly employed, with brick-red as an alternative, both of them varying in tone and clarity according to the accuracy of the firing; the former could vary from a pure black to a dull green or a blackish-

Above: Globular shaped creamware teapot, circa 1770, with hand-enamelled Chinoiserie design in the Rhodes style. The moulded cabbage spout and rope twist handle are distinctive Wedgwood features

Opposite: Creamware coffee pot, circa 1775, with shell edge, plume finial and twist handle, decorated with a red transfer print of 'Liverpool Birds' by Sadler and Green

Above: *Creamware radish dish, circa 1765–70, with free hand-painted botanical central motif and 'Husk' border. In 1770 the Empress Catherine II ordered a service in this design*

brown. From 1770 a further colour, purple, was sometimes used.

Sadler and Green worked for Wedgwood from 1761. Once a fortnight Wedgwood sent down by carrier a load of creamware to be printed, the waggon returning with the next consignment of completed ware. An invoice of 11 April 1764 shows that Wedgwood paid the Liverpool firm about £65 for decorating 1,730 pieces of ware, the list comprising 'Teapots in three sizes, Mugs in two sizes, Bowls, all sizes, Coffee Pots, Sugars, Cream Ewers, and Cups and Saucers'.

Printing, whatever the colour, gave the pottery a sophistication that enabled it to vie on artistic grounds with porcelain, while the cost of the finished articles was much less. In a particular instance of decorative treatment there was little or nothing to choose in appearance between creamware, delftware and porcelain. This was when a pattern painted or printed in black was overlaid with a wash of transparent green which allowed the basic design to show through. Wedgwood's successful use of transfer-printing on creamware is seen on page 36, which shows a dish from a dessert service of *c.* 1775.

Thomas Bentley

Wedgwood often visited Liverpool where not only did he see Sadler and Green about decorating, but he also had calls to make respecting export of his wares to America and the Indies. On the occasion of a visit there in the middle of 1762 he damaged his already injured knee and the local surgeon, Mathew Turner, ordered him to rest. Perhaps to alleviate the boredom of his patient, Turner introduced one of his friends, Thomas Bentley, whom he brought with him to the inn where Wedgwood was detained. 'Bentley', wrote Miss Meteyard, 'came forward with his gallant bow and courtly manner, took the kindly proffered hand, looked into the good and strongly expressive face of the Staffordshire potter; and from this moment, these men were more than brothers.'

Bentley was a partner in the local firm of Bentley and Boardman, merchants, and had been born in Derbyshire in 1730, the same year as Wedgwood. He had a wide range of intellectual interests, enjoyed the friendship of many talented men of the north-west, and was a Unitarian: a Dissenter, whose religious beliefs were combined with a radical political allegiance. His views coincided with those of his new acquaintance, although Bentley's education was superior.

As soon as he had recovered sufficiently to stand the journey, Wedgwood returned to Burslem and hard work. There is no doubt that he was still experimenting to improve his output in quality and quantity, and was still di-

Above: Portrait of Thomas Bentley by Joseph Wright of Derby, circa 1778. Bentley was Wedgwood's partner from August 1769 until his death in November 1780

recting his attention principally to creamware. At this date it was still of a deep colour, but no mark was used, and the principal evidence as to its tint comes from a letter of rather later date when he had perfected his pale cream colour. In 1768 Wedgwood wrote about his 'endeavour to make it as pale as possible . . . but it is impossible that any one colour, even though it were to come down from Heaven, should please every taste'.

Above: Green-painted, black transfer fruit dish. Much of the transfer printing introduced as an alternative to painting was done in black on Wedgwood ware

Left: Creamware vase, circa 1770, an example of early unmarked Wedgwood. The vase was engine turned and has an artichoke finial

The next event in Josiah's life was a domestic one: he married his cousin, Sarah, daughter of Richard Wedgwood, a cheese-merchant of Smallwood, east Cheshire, in the church at Astbury, Cheshire, on 25 January.

A year later, on 3 January 1765, Josiah celebrated the birth of the first of his nine children, a daughter who was named Susannah. After she had been baptised, her father wrote to his eldest brother John that 'we have now added another Christian to the family . . . Sukey is a fine sprightly lass, & will bear a good deal of dandleing & you can sing —

lullaby Baby — whilst I rock the Cradle . . .' It suggests a pretty scene of brotherly accord, and reveals that Josiah was not so preoccupied with the pottery as to be immune to the joys of parenthood.

Some valuable commissions

For some time past Josiah had made use of his brother, John, who lived in the city of London, in Cateaton Street, almost opposite the Guildhall. He was conveniently situated to act as a part-time agent for his brother in Staffordshire, arranging such things as sending him supplies of gold powder for gilding, seeing engravers for the making of copperplates, and paying visits to clients who resided in the capital.

It was to John that he wrote in mid-June, 1765. He began:

Dear Brother
I'll teach you to find fault, & scold,
& grumble at my not writing, I
warrant you, & as to your going to

France, I do not believe I can spare you out of London this summer, if business comes in for you at this rate, for instance — An ord^r. from St. James's for a service of Staffordshire ware, about which I want to ask a hundred questions, & have never a mouth but yours in Town worth opening upon the subject.

The ord^r. came from Miss Deborah alias De^b. Chetwynd, sempstress, & Laundress to the Queen, to Mr. Smallw^d. of Newcastle, who bro^t. it to me (I believe because nobody else w^d. undertake it) & is as follows.

A complete sett of tea things, with a gold ground and raised flowers upon it in green, in the same manner of the green flowers that are raised upon the mehons, so it is wrote but I suppose it sho^d. be melons — The articles are 12 cups for Tea, & 12 Saucers a slop bason, sugar dish wth. cover & stand, Teapot & stand, spoon trea, Coffeepot, 12 Coffee cups, 6 p^r. of hand candlesticks & 6 Mellons with leaves. 6 green fruit baskets & stands edged with gold.

Left: Wedgwood Queensware tureen and cover with a view of Shugborough, Staffordshire

In a postscript he added with understandable excitement: 'Pray put on *the best suit of Cloaths you ever had in your life,* & take the first opportunity of going to Court. Miss Chetwynd is Daughter to the Master of the Mint.'

It is sad to record that there remains no other evidence of this service, every single item of it having vanished over the years. Nevertheless, this order from Buckingham House (as it was then named) gave him exactly the encouragement he needed.

Engine-turned wares

Wedgwood was spending some of his time experimenting with the lathe, a tool not unknown in potteries in its elementary form for giving prefired wares a smooth finish. He realised that the more complicated machine used for ornamenting ivory, wood, and metal had an untapped potential for decorating pottery. An engine-turning lathe was adapted for the work and found satisfactory, giving wares an attractive and distinctive appearance.

Many of the improvements and modifications to the lathe were executed for Wedgwood by John Wyke of Liverpool, who specialised in watchmakers' tools and was a friend of Bentley.

In a letter to his brother in London, sent a month after the one previously quoted, the successful use of the lathe is mentioned. John made contact with Miss Chetwynd, and as a result Wedgwood had received permission to send some of his wares for inspection by Queen Charlotte. The relevant paragraph reads:

> *I shall be very proud of the honour of sending a box of patterns to the Queen, amongst which I intend sending two setts of Vases, Cream colour-engine turn'd, and printed, for which purpose nothing could be more suitable than some copper plates I have by me.*

Vases with engine-turned ornament in the shape of closely spaced wavy ribs and flutes, but without any printing on them, have been recorded in the dark-toned creamware of the period, and it is reasonable to assume that they are similar to those referred to in the letter.

Writing to Cateaton Street at the end of July or beginning of August 1765 (the letter is undated), Wedgwood detailed some of his difficulties in finishing the teaset for the Queen. The gilding was proving very troublesome, and he suggested that John should ask the advice of a man named Jinks who had worked at Chelsea and was then at Bow. The letter closed with a paragraph of local news of special interest to the writer:

> *Dr. Swan dined with Lord Gower this week; after dinner your Brother Josiah's Pottworks were the subject of conversation for some time, the Cream colour Table services in particular. I believe it was his Lordship said that nothing of the sort could exceed them for a fine glaze, &c.*

Lord Gower had been appointed Lord Lieutenant of Staffordshire in 1755, and successively held a number of important posts.

The Trent and Mersey canal scheme

In March 1765 a long-mooted scheme for a canal to link Liverpool and Hull by way of north Staffordshire was revived, and Wedgwood rallied his fellow-potters in a cause which was bound to benefit the entire district. He certainly had no doubts that such a canal would assist his business, and the trade of other potters, in the same way as the earlier turnpike had done.

His friend Thomas Bentley participated in the project, and another close friend, Dr Erasmus Darwin of Lichfield, physician and poet, also played a part; the two men were responsible for composing a pamphlet for distribution by Wedgwood. As might be expected, Lord Gower became associated with the plan and the Duke of Bridgewater, whose engineer, James Brindley, had already constructed more than one canal, was no less involved.

In May 1766 Wedgwood was appointed treasurer by the Proprietors of the Navigation from the Trent to the Mersey, the body formed to carry through the project.

In addition to expediting the carriage of goods, the preliminaries with which Wedgwood was so closely concerned enlarged his clientele in more than one direction. In a letter of 6 July he wrote to John:

I should have wrote to you sooner but have been waiting upon his G- the D- of Bridgewater with plans &c. respecting Inland Navigation. Mr Sparrow [solicitor, of Newcastle-under-Lyme] went along with me, we were most graciously rec^d. spent about 8 hours in his G-'s comp^y., & had all the assurances of his concurrence with our designs that we could wish. His G- gave me an ord^r. for the completest Table service of Cream colour that I could make . . .

Again, he wrote to Bentley in October 1765 telling of business in hand which was doubtless owed to the good offices of Lord Gower:

I have been three Days hard & close at work takeing patt^{ns}. from a set of French China at the Duke of Bedford's, worth at least £1,500, the most elegant things I ever saw.

The service in question, of Sèvres porcelain, had been presented to the Duchess by Louis XV in 1763 when the Duke of Bedford was British Ambassador at Paris. Each piece was richly painted with panels of flowers or exotic birds reserved on a dark blue and gilt ground, and it remains to this day at Woburn Abbey. Josiah would have been less interested in the decoration of the

Opposite: *Engine-turned Wedgwood creamware vase and cover. Engine-turning could result in considerable variety of distinctive ornamentation*

Above: *Engraving from Josiah Wedgwood's 1774 creamware catalogue of a preserves dish, adapted from one in the Duke of Bedford's Sèvres porcelain service*

service than in the shapes of the numerous items, and J.V.G. Mallet has drawn attention to a creamware dish (in the Victoria and Albert Museum) closely resembling that beneath the Sèvres soup tureen. The preserves dish, which was engraved in Wedgwood's 1774 catalogue, was certainly inspired by a *confiturier* also emanating from the same source.

A London showroom

In the summer of 1765 Wedgwood became concerned about the transaction of business in the capital. In August he wrote tactfully to his brother, who was apparently retired, inquiring whether he could devote more of his time to representing the Burslem manufactory. Wedgwood had clearly determined to enter into competition with porcelain by extending his output to include vases and other purely decorative articles, while not neglecting the market for tableware. It was by no means unreasonable that he should do

so, for his cream-coloured pottery supplanted the delftware which in its day had embraced both categories of goods. He foresaw that London would be the place in which to sell both vases and services, especially the former, and he was reinforced in his opinion a week later. Then, he wrote to John that he had had a visit at Burslem from the Duke of Marlborough, Lord Gower, Lord Spencer 'and others', who made some purchases and remarked that they wondered why he had not got a London warehouse.

Soon afterwards two events occurred: a couple of rooms were rented in Mayfair, in Charles Street (now Carlos Place), and John left London to live in Liverpool. Someone must therefore be found to attend to the new premises and its clients, and Wedgwood sent William Cox. The fact that this man was a bookkeeper at Burslem suggests that selling goods was considered to be less important than the rendering of accounts and collecting of monies outstanding; bad debts were a notorious feature of the business world in 18th-century London, and all too frequently led to bankruptcy.

It was in the summer of 1766 that Queen Charlotte appointed Wedgwood 'Potter to Her Majesty'. Shortly afterwards he began to refer to his pottery as 'Queensware' and his London address became 'The Queen's Arms'. At a later date he reconsidered the matter, advertising it primarily as his 'Warehouse', the reason being 'that the *Queens Arms* may not be thought to be a Tavern'.

During the busy time when he was

engaged in assisting in the promotion of the Trent and Mersey canal, fulfilling the Queen's order and worrying about representation in London, Wedgwood was also energetically pursuing plans to expand his pottery. As early as March 1765 he told his brother about experiments he was making with a whiter body and glaze. Then he wrote: 'I do not intend to make this ware at Burslem & am therefore laying out for an agreeable situation elsewhere.' The 'situation elsewhere' eventually proved to be an estate of 350 acres, the Ridge House estate, a few miles to the south of Burslem and just to the north-east of Newcastle-under-Lyme.

Early in the summer of 1767 Wedgwood and Bentley agreed to become partners in the new venture. The potter had been pressing for this to take place, but was well aware that it meant Bentley would have to leave Liverpool and all his friends there.

Building a new pottery

Erection of the new manufactory began under the direction of a Derby architect and builder, Joseph Pickford, who built at the same time a house apiece for the two partners; over one hundred dwellings were also provided for employees. Wedgwood was eager that his pottery should be as up-to-date and efficient as possible, and the plans for it incorporated some of the features of the Soho engineering workshops at Birmingham that had opened in 1765. The owner of Soho, Matthew Boulton, was admired by Wedgwood who described him as 'very ingenious, philosophical,

Above: *White on pale blue jasper portrait medallion of Queen Charlotte, Wedgwood's patroness who gave her title to Queensware, in an ormulu frame*

and agreeable', both men having much in common as regards their approach to industrialisation.

While his new factory was under construction, Wedgwood was far from idle, spending some of his time developing a new variety of pottery suitable for forming into vases and other decorative objects. For this, he took the local black

Above: *Wedgwood creamware large tureen and sauce tureen, circa 1775–80, decorated with free hand-enamelled patterns of 'Laurel' and 'Pink Antique'*

Egyptian, and in due course produced a finely grained hard black pottery, referred to at the time as 'Etruscan'. The first successful vases made from the new material were completed and sent to Bentley at the end of August 1768, and at the same time Wedgwood was still busily experimenting with vases made from his creamware.

The creamware vases imitated in shape and decoration prototypes of stone and marble, reflecting a taste among connoisseurs for exotic natural stones, a taste that was especially pre-valent in France. Many of Wedgwood's creamware versions were made with ornamental moulding, swags and handles, gilded in imitation of the metalwork on the French originals. The gilding has proved unable to withstand the wear-and-tear of two centuries, and the unadorned cream-coloured pottery is now revealed, so that the rich appearance of the vases can only be imagined.

Although their manufacture was initiated before Wedgwood moved into his new premises, most surviving examples of the creamware vases were made there. The earlier specimens were decorated with painting on the surface and may, generally speaking, be distinguished from those of later date. These were made of semi-blended coloured clays, and were veined throughout the material in the manner of the old Staffordshire agate ware.

Once again Wedgwood was troubled about his London representation, this time with the emphasis on selling.

> . . . to enable me to show various Table and dessert services completely set out on two ranges of Tables, six or eight at least such services are absolutely necessary to be shewn in order to **do the needful** with the Ladys in the neatest, genteelest & best method. The same, or indeed a much greater variety of setts of Vases sho[d]. decorate the Walls, & both these articles may, every few days, be so alter'd, revers'd, & transform'd as to render the whole a new scene, even to the same Company, every time they bring their friends to visit us. I need not tell you the many good effects this may produce, when business, & amusement can be made to go hand in hand. Every new show, Exhibition, or rarity soon goes stale in London, & is no longer regarded after the first sight, unless utility or some such variety as I have hinted at above continue to recommend it to their notice.

Clients, he continued, would cease to call and bring their friends if the display remained unaltered:

> This may be avoided by us with very little address, when we have a Room proper for the purpose. I have done something of the sort since I came to Town & find the immediate good Effects of it. The first two days after the alteration we sold three complete setts of Vases at 2 & 3 Guineas a sett, besides many pairs of them, which Vases had been in my Rooms 6–8 & some of them 12 months, & wanted nothing but arrangement to sell them.

Within a few days he thought he had found what he wanted in Westminster and again in Pall Mall, the latter premises having been used for auction sales, but both were rejected for one reason or another.

Then, in the spring of 1768 he was again in London, and on 24 March wrote to Bentley announcing that he had taken the lease of a house in St Martin's Lane, and had already engaged a china-painter 'just come out of Yorkshire', conjectured to be David Rhodes of Leeds, who would in due course be accommodated at the new address. Hardly had this letter been sent when, just a week later, another followed to notify a change of plan: 'I have met with another house which pleases me better than that I have taken.' The second of these was No. 1 Great Newport Street, at the top of St Martin's Lane, and after negotiations had been concluded the showroom was opened to the public in August of that year.

In addition to all his pressing preoccupations in Burslem and London, Josiah was not free from personal anxiety. His brother John, on a visit to London in June 1767, had been to Ranelagh Gardens and after watching the fireworks display called at the Swan Inn at Westminster Bridge. He left there at midnight and nothing further

was known of his movements until 5 a.m. when his body was recovered from the Thames. Josiah was very affected by this sad event, being as he wrote to a friend 'rather too susceptible to grief'. John was nine years senior to Josiah, and forty-six years of age when he died.

Just a year later, Wedgwood found that his right leg was increasingly giving him pain. He made up his mind to have it amputated prior to the opening of the new pottery, the operation being performed on 28 May 1768. He recovered quickly, and within a short time was hard at work again.

Vases continued to be an exciting preoccupation, and once the black ones were perfected their manufacture began at the Bell Works. Production could not keep pace with demand. It would be no exaggeration to say that Wedgwood was then living in a wonderland of vases and

was almost in a state of obsession with them. In his own words: 'I have lately had a vision by night of some new Vases, Tablets &c. with wch. Articles we shall certainly serve the *whole World.*'

Above: View of Wedgwood's Etruria factory, taken around 1930, showing the cupola (Bell Tower); ***Opposite:*** *Group of transfer-printed Queensware, circa 1770–80;* ***Back:*** *Queen's Shape Plate, decorated with black transfer-print of ruins, inspired by Paul Sandby;*
Centre: *coffee pot decorated with iron-red transfer-print, inspired by Gainsborough's 'Rural Lovers';*
Left: *teacup and saucer with moulded shell edge, rope-twist handle and red transfer-print of 'Liverpool Birds';*
Right: *teapoy decorated with black transfer-print*

Black basalt Etruscan vase, circa 1780, with swan's head handles

Chapter Three

ETRURIA I

With the rapid expansion of his business, Wedgwood outgrew the Bell Works and in 1769 moved to a new factory. Its inauguration was marked by six commemorative 'First Day' Etruscan vases, and the factory was named Etruria after these. It was here that the finest vases and other ornamental wares associated with the name of Wedgwood were to be produced. These included a 1000-piece table service for the Empress Catherine of Russia, a commission which brought Wedgwood immense prestige. As from the early 1770s, too, Wedgwood developed a keen interest in cameos and medallions, which became a lucrative side of his business.

Left: *Inscription side of one of six 'First Day' vases, of which only four survive, thrown by Josiah Wedgwood himself to commemorate the opening of the Etruria factory on 13 June 1769. Wedgwood Museum, Barlaston*

Left: *Inscription side of one of six 'First Day' vases, of which only four survive, thrown by Josiah Wedgwood himself to commemorate the opening of the Etruria factory on 13 June 1769. Wedgwood Museum, Barlaston*

Opposite: *Decorative side of the basalt Etruscan 'First Day' vase shown on the left. Wedgwood Museum, Barlaston*

In 1769 all that related to vase-making was transferred from the Bell Works to the new manufactory, which was opened ceremonially on 13 June. To mark the occasion the partners made six Etruscan vases, with covers and upright handles, Wedgwood performing the throwing while Bentley provided motive power for the wheel. The vases were sent to London for painting with classical figures above the words '*Artes Etruriae Renascuntur*' ('The Arts of Etruria are revived') with a commemorative inscription on the other side.

In honour of the area of Italy where the much-admired pottery vases were thought to have originated, the estate and factory were named 'Etruria', Wedgwood's new house being Etruria Hall and Bentley's the more prosaic Bank House. The Etruscan objects, although excavated in the part of north Italy known as Etruria, were later found to have been imported there from Greece, but this fact was not accepted until after the building and naming of the manufactory had taken place.

The Hamilton collection

The subjects selected for the decoration of the First Day Vases were taken from a book illustrating ancient vases belonging to William (later Sir William) Hamilton who had assembled more than one outstanding collection of vases.

Another key source was the '*Receuil d'antiquités égyptiennes, étrusques, gréques, romaines, et gauloises*' by the Comte de Caylus, published in six volumes at Paris between 1752 and 1767. Wedgwood

was loaned a copy of the work; then he and Bentley purchased one for their own use. From time to time they acquired other books illustrating ancient vases and antiquities, many of which inspired the shapes and decoration of Etruria's productions.

The partnership between Josiah Wedgwood and Thomas Bentley related only to Etruria and the goods intended for manufacture there, Bentley having no financial interest in the tablewares and other 'useful' articles being produced at the Bell Works. In September 1770 the distinctions to be drawn regarding the output of the two places were still the subject of discussion between the two men, and Wedgwood wrote:

> With respect to the difference between **Usefull ware & Ornamental** I do not find any inclination in myself to be over nice in drawing the line. You know I never had any idea that the **Ornamental ware** sho^d. not be of 'some use'.

The writer then referred to a query by Bentley as to whether his friend's other partnership, that with Thomas Wedgwood at the Bell Works, precluded the making of 'Stellas ewers' at Etruria; the ewers in question being copied from a

Left: *Basalt vase and cover, circa 1775, the encaustic decoration copied from an engraving of a vase in the possession of Sir William Hamilton. Castle Museum, Nottingham*

design in the *Livre de vases* by Jacques Stella, a painter and engraver who lived from 1595 to 1657. Several paragraphs of argument followed, with Wedgwood summing-up his ideas in these words:

> May not usefull ware be comprehended under this simple definition, of such vessels as are **made use of at meals**. This appears to me the most simple & natural line & though it does not take in Wash-hand basons & bottles or Ewers & a few such articles, they are of little consequence & speak plain enough for themselves; nor wo^d. this exclude such superb vessels for sideboards, or vases for desserts if they could be introduc'd, as these articles wo^d. be rather for **shew** than **use**.

A footnote in Bentley's handwriting on the original letter indicates that thenceforward all was well: 'The Difficulty was easily settled . . . '

The Etruscan vases

The vases excavated in northern Italy were decorated in red on a black ground, or vice versa, by a method that had become forgotten by the 18th century. For imitating them it was necessary to develop some suitable enamels that would emerge from the kiln with little or none of the customary gloss. Wedgwood experimented to produce pigments that remained matt, while he worked also on a glaze to simulate bronze. Both goals were finally attained, and in November 1769 Wedgwood was granted a patent for 'The purpose of ornamenting earthen and

porcelaine ware with an encaustic gold bronze, together with a peculiar species of encaustic painting in various colours, in imitation of the ancient Etruscan and Roman earthenware'. The use of the term 'encaustic' in the circumstances was confusing, as although the word means literally 'burnt-in' it was, and is, normally applied to the ancient method of painting on a panel with coloured waxes that were melted into the wood.

A Hanley potter, Humphrey Palmer, was soon found to be marketing his own versions of decorated black vases comparable to those of Wedgwood. The latter took out an injunction against the pirate; in the end an agreement was reached and the action withdrawn, but the occurrence was only one among numerous cases when others profited unfairly from Wedgwood's innovations.

Although arrangements had been made for Bentley to live in a house built at Etruria, he never did so. Instead, in September 1769 a house was leased at Chelsea where he was to live and superintend a group of painters, who would decorate the wares sent down from Staffordshire. The success of his vases was even greater than Wedgwood

Above: *large round framed plaque of 'Herculaneum Dancer', circa 1774. These plaques were used as architectural features. Traces of the original gilding can still be seen*

Opposite: *Portrait of Sir William Hamilton, studio of Sir Joshua Reynolds*

anticipated and for a while there were worries over finding a sufficient number of competent and reliable painters for employment at Chelsea. The porcelain factories furnished a few, including Ralph and Catherine Wilcox. Mrs Wilcox was the daughter of Thomas Frye, one-time manager of the Bow Porcelain factory, but she was not anxious to return to the capital after having worked in the country at Worcester. 'I must talk to her again', wrote Wedgwood on 20 September 1769, and as a consequence of his persuasion the Wilcoxes went to Chelsea. Bentley was informed on the same occasion, 'I hired an ingenious Boy last night for Etruria as a Modeler'. The latter was William Hackwood, who stayed with the factory until 1832.

Although the Etruscan vases were then so prominent, if only because they were something entirely new, creamware (alias crystalline, variegated or pebble) continued in production. Early in 1770 Wedgwood defined them to Bentley as follows:

> *Pebble vases. Suppose we call those barely sprinkled with blue and ornaments gilt, **granite**; when veined with black, **veined granite**; with gold, **lapis lazuli**; with colours and veined, **variegated pebble**; those with colours, and veined without any blue sprinkling, **Egyptian pebble**.*

On another occasion he referred to 'Holy Door' and 'Jaune Antique'. Miss Meteyard wrote that the first-named was supposed to be a rich mixture of light puce or mauve varied by gold and white, and the second a rich saffron and black. She attempted to clarify the situation with a brief list:

Serpentine   Grey and green

Agate   Brown and yellow, with sometimes grey and white

Verde antique   Dark green, grey and black

Green jasper   Green and grey

Grey granite   White and black

Red porphry   White on red

Wedgwood was still busy with his tablewares, ensuring that they were up to his standards and that orders were filled promptly. He was anxious to increase the sale of the whole range of goods, remarking to Bentley in August 1770: 'We are looking over the English Peerage to find out *lines & connections* — will you look over the Irish Peerage with the same view — I need not tell you how much will depend upon a *proper & noble* introduction.' He knew that if royalty and the nobility approved of his wares, then everyone else would demand them. In the same year building began at Etruria so that the making of useful wares could be transferred from the Bell Works, and all activities would be under the one roof.

Many of the vases, whether creamware or Etruscan, were mounted on bases of black or white pottery or, occasionally, of marble. Each article was affixed to its base by means of an iron or brass threaded post with a flat top and a nut to hold all firm. Miss Meteyard mentioned that the metal parts were sometimes sent down to the capital from Etruria, and that 'a man named Palethorpe also effected much of this work in London, and charged from 6d. to 1s. 6d. for fixing vases and plinths together . . . '

Decorated tableware

The painting-shop at Chelsea did not confine its activities to vases and ornamental pieces, but also decorated tablewares. Jewitt owned and printed a list of payments made to painters employed there in October 1770, the two cash columns headed 'On J.W.'s Acct.' and 'On W. & B.'s Acct.', thus making it clear that pieces from the Bell Works were treated quite separately from those of Etruria.

Crests

A series of simple patterns evolved over the years for the ornamentation of services, plates and other items being given borders of Etruscan derivation with repeats of such motifs as anthemions or husks. Alternatively there were flower, fruit and leaf designs that are no less reflective of the taste of the period and of Josiah himself. Crests with or without full coats of arms were added to order, only occasionally being placed centrally, as was so often the case with imported Chinese porcelain. It says much for the creamware that plates, dishes and other tablewares could be produced in their tens of thousands, and that they could be sold with a minimum of coloured decoration; their appeal lay basically in the excellent shaping that was both functional and attractive, and in the unblemished glaze.

The Russian table service

In 1768 Lord Cathcart was appointed Ambassador-Extraordinary to the Empress Catherine of Russia. Wedgwood received orders to supply dinner and dessert services bearing the Cathcart crest. He informed Bentley that 'I have spent several hours with L^d. Cathcart our Ambassador to Russia, & we are to do great things for each other'. The Empress and many of her wealthy sub-

jects made extensive purchases of tablewares and other goods, and in late 1773 Catherine began to negotiate through her Consul in London, Alexander Baxter, for a very large and elaborately decorated table service. The whole was to comprise nearly 1,000 pieces, each to be decorated with a view in England and to bear the crest of a frog; the latter denoting that it was for use at the Chesmenski Palace, which was in an area known as La Grenouillière (once called the Frog-marsh), near Leningrad.

Above: *Examples of Wedgwood armorial ware*

Overleaf (left): *Wedgwood jasper vase and cover, circa 1790, with relief of 'The Apotheosis of Homer', designed by Flaxman*

Overleaf (right): *A selection of various Wedgwood jasper ornaments. These are solid blue and white jasper cameos mounted in cut steel (probably made by Matthew Boulton of the Soho Works, Birmingham)*

Above: *Portrait of the Empress Catherine II by Giovanni-Battista Lampi, 1793*

Wedgwood was delighted to have received such an important commission, but cautiously discussed with his partner the enormous amount of work involved and its cost. He was also anxious about the fate of the order if a war or some political upheaval should occur suddenly in Russia before the account had been settled. In the end it

was decided that the potential advertising value of the service was so great that the risk was worth taking.

Designing the service

The painting of the many pieces and the selection of the subjects were the basis of much correspondence between Staffordshire and London. A few samples were decorated with the principal scene in full colour, but it was quickly found that the cost would be prohibitive, and a colour described variously as 'mulberry', 'delicate black' and 'purple' was adopted for the views. The frog, painted a bright green, was placed in the border at the top. The partners wondered whether each view should be purposely drawn, but Wedgwood saw the impossibility of this, asking:

> *Do you think the subjects must be all from real views and real Buildings, & that it is expected from us to send draftsmen all over the kingdom. . . ?*

In July (1773) it was decided that Wedgwood should have sketches made of suitable buildings and views in the vicinity of Etruria, and he told Bentley that he had had the offer of a loan of 'Wilson's views from different places in Wales'.

However, the principal source was engravings, of which there was no shortage and that were easy for the decorators to copy.

The great service was completed in the middle of 1774, and before its dispatch to Russia was placed on display to the public at the London showroom.

The premises in Greek Street, known as Portland House because the ground landlords were the Dukes of Portland, were leased by the firm to replace both the showroom in Great Newport Street and the painting-shop in Chelsea. Portland House was opened with the exhibition of the Russian service which lasted for two months from 1 June 1774. In July, Bentley moved to 11 Greek Street, adjoining Portland House, where he was well placed to give his attention to all departments of the London end of the

Above: Russian service plates, depicting view at Castle Acre, Norfolk, with frog crest picked out in green and Aysgarth Bridge, Yorkshire, decorated in polychrome enamels

partnership, which were now under one roof.

Wedgwood wrote to his partner early in July saying he was glad to learn that the service was being prepared for packing. He then turned to the business of payment, hoping Bentley would be careful not to omit any of the numerous expenses incurred that were unforeseen when the initial estimate was compiled.

In due course the service reached its destination and the bill for it was paid. The cost to the Empress is unknown, but has been calculated to have been approximately £2,700, to which the actual unpainted pottery contributed a mere £51 8s. 4d. Although the makers may have made only a small immediate profit in money terms, unquestionably they derived long-lasting benefit from the publicity surrounding the commission. Interest was aroused not only by the service itself, its appearance and magnitude, but by the notoriety of its buyer. Exhibiting the entire service in London at the height of the Season was a good stroke of business.

In 1779, Sir James Harris, British Ambassador at St. Petersburg, noted in his diary how favourably he was treated by the Empress. On one occasion she took him on a visit to La Grenouillière and showed him the Wedgwood service. It then vanished from record until 1909, when Dr G.C. Williamson devoted a book to its description and illustration. At the time of publication, Tsar Nicholas II permitted a number of pieces to come to London to be shown publicly at premises in Conduit Street. Afterwards these speciments were returned to Russia, but it has been suggested that a few of them somehow failed to do so, or that they 'escaped' during or soon after the Revolution. There survive also in the West a few of the trials painted in full colour, and others decorated in monochrome, but

lacking the frog crest. A portion of the original service is now housed in the Hermitage at Leningrad.

The 1773 catalogue

The year before the Russian service was finished saw the publication of a sixty-page catalogue of Wedgwood and Bentley's productions. The title page announced its contents:

A Catalogue of Cameos, Intaglios, Medals and Bas Reliefs, with a general account of Vases and other ornaments after the antique; made by Wedgwood and Bentley, and sold at their rooms in Great Newport Street, London.

The introduction included descriptions of the different types of pottery resulting from Josiah's ceaseless trials, many of them made in the few years following the opening of Etruria.

*To give an idea of the **nature** and **variety** of the productions of our ornamental works, it will be necessary to point out and describe the various **compositions** of which the forms, &c., are made, and to distinguish and arrange the several productions in suitable **classes**.*

*The **compositions**, or bodies, of which the ornamental pieces are made, may be divided into the following branches:-*

Opposite: *Queensware pierced orange bowl, circa 1770, first illustrated in the Wedgwood Catalogue of 1774*

*I. A composition of **terra-cotta**, resembling porphyry, lapis lazuli, jasper, and other beautiful stones, of the vitrescent or crystalline class.*

*II. A fine **black porcelain**, having nearly the same properties as the **basaltes**, resisting the attacks of acids, being a touchstone to copper, silver, and gold, and equal in hardness to agate or porphyry.*

*III. A fine white biscuit ware, or **terra-cotta**, polished and unpolished.*

The term 'terra-cotta' was used as literally translated, meaning baked earth, and the vases in Class I were the creamware ones described earlier. The 'black porcelain' of Class II was the hard pottery used for making Etruscan vases and other articles, which were described henceforward as 'basaltes'. The 'white biscuit' of Class III was the white counterpart to the preceding and was also left unglazed; it and the basaltes could be polished by a lapidary.

Two other compositions produced from *c.* 1775 onwards were caneware, which was buff-coloured and was finished with and without a glaze; and rosso antico, which was a terra-cotta

red and was more often than not glazeless. These and others when finished in the biscuit or unglazed state were known as 'Dry' bodies.

Cameos and medallions

Since early in the 1770s a fresh field had been increasingly occupying Josiah's attention: cameos or gems, and ornamental tablets and medallions. The tablets were, as stated in the 1773 catalogue, for insetting in chimney-pieces and furniture. Alison Kelly in *Decorative Wedgwood* illustrates some

Opposite: *Three early Wedgwood engine-turned vases, circa 1765, with two matching stands, of deep-tinted creamware. All are unmarked.*

Above right: *Wedgwood canopic jar, circa 1790, of rosso antico, with black decoration*

Above: *Plate from Wedgwood Illustrated Sales Catalogue, 1774, showing amongst other things a sauce tureen lid, stand and ladle, creamers of varying forms and a leafage candlestick*

pieces of the years 1775-80, among them a *bonheur du jour* or lady's writing-table, heavily inlaid with cameos that are almost certainly of basaltes with painted backgrounds and painted relief figures. More successful in design is a set of eight armchairs once in the Library at Appuldurcombe Park, Isle of Wight, which are of Greek-inspired pattern, each of the top-rails being centred in a small Etruscan portrait medallion depicting a writer.

Ancient carved stone cameos, or gems as they were termed alternatively, had for a long time been eagerly sought by connoisseurs.

Wedgwood began by making his cameos from the basaltes with which he had so successfully made his Etruscan vases; he had first tried them in 1769 as ornaments on the latter, terming them 'Medallion Vases'. The 1773 catalogue listed no fewer than 285 different cameos and their counterparts, intaglios, which had their ornament incised instead of in relief and were therefore usable as seals.

The sale of small cameos for mounting as jewellery had grown into a profitable side of the business. The seals, which could be used for sealing letters and were often carried on the person in the way of a dress accessory, were usually of basaltes polished on the wheel. The cameos were sometimes of the same material, or else of the white biscuit listed in the catalogue.

Designs for the intaglios and cameos came from many sources. At first, the majority originated in those produced by James Tassie, a Scottish gem-engraver who began life as a stone-mason. Wedgwood also made his own moulds from original gems belonging to collectors like the Duke of Marlborough. The range of subjects of the portrait cameos widened with the years, and by 1787, when the sixth edition of the catalogue was published, they included a large number of personages of all periods: mythological figures, poets, painters, royalty and most of Wedgwood's patrons. They could be purchased in sets, singly, or complete with cabinets designed and made to hold them. Each item, cameo or intaglio, was sold enclosed in a paper printed with the name of the subject represented and the catalogue number.

Portrait busts

At Etruria a further use was found for basaltes in the making of ancient and contemporary portrait busts. When carved in marble or cast in plaster these were popular in libraries.

As with the cameos, a start was made by buying ready-made examples, in this instance made of plaster, supplied by James Hoskins, moulder and caster in plaster to the Royal Academy, and his partners Samuel Euclid Oliver and Benjamin Grant.

Although always occupied with his

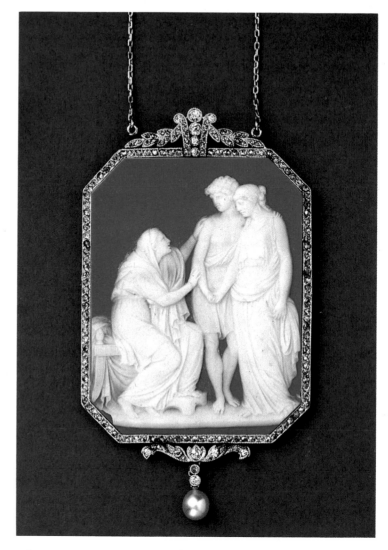

Above: *Edwardian diamond-mounted Wedgwood plaque*

experiments, Wedgwood did not neglect the staple profit-earner, creamware. As early as 1767-8 he had the idea of preparing a quantity of samples to send to dealers and agents, and this was continued for many years. The samples took the form of wooden boxes fitted with internal divisions to hold seven or more plates of different sizes and shapes with varying border patterns. Each box was accompanied by a detailed price-list and a set of engravings showing the various articles currently obtainable. Fresh products were tried if they appeared likely to be profitable. These included cisterns for water closets, although none have survived.

As long ago as 1771 a showroom had been opened in Dublin, and was managed by a man named Brock for a number of years. Good business was done there at the start, but this fell off and the enterprise then caused continual anxiety. The year after the opening of the Dublin premises, Bentley went to Bath to seek a suitable outlet there and settled on some rooms in Westgate Buildings.

In June 1772 Wedgwood took his wife, who had been seriously ill, to Bath for the waters and the change of air. While he was there he wrote to Bentley requesting him to send down a further supply for their showroom as it was essential for the firm to exhibit a complete selection of their ware, 'or we had better do nothing for I think the Toy, & China shops are richer and more extravagant in their shew here than in London.'

Problems with the workforce

Sarah Wedgwood made a slow recovery, but Josiah suffered anxieties not only on account of his wife's illness and his own disability. His employees and their grievances contributed their share. The men started to complain about the piece-rates they were receiv-

ing, which Wedgwood had decided before he left for Bath were too high in view of the changed state of trade: sales of vases showed a severe drop, and, as he put it in a letter of 23 August 1772:

The Great People have had their Vases in their Palaces long enough for them to be seen and admir'd, by the **Middling Class** *of People, which Class we know are vastly, I had almost said infinitely, superior in number, to the Great, & though a* **great price** *was I believe at first necessary to make the Vases esteemed* **Ornaments for Palaces** *that reason no longer exists. Their character is established, & the middling People would probably buy quantitys of them at a reduced price.*

Wedgwood pointed out that overheads ran on unabated and the only way in which he could reduce his expenses and lower the price of his goods was by 'making the greatest quantity possible in a given time'. Bentley would have understood the argument, but it was far from easy to convince the workers that if they produced more at a lower rate per item their overall wages would not be reduced.

There was trouble, too, in London, where the head clerk, Benjamin Mather, was reported by an anonymous correspondent to have been embezzling the firm's money. Wedgwood had been suspicious of him because his accounts were always behindhand, and for some months he did not appear to have drawn his wages although he must have had money from somewhere. Instant dis-

missal was ruled out: 'he may go and collect thousands from our Creditors'. A week later Wedgwood wrote:

I shall be very glad, as well on the young man's account as my own, to know that he has not gone any great lengths in either vice or youthful folly . . .

The matter continued to be discussed by the partners, Josiah considering that it would be wrong to discharge Mather peremptorily, and it would be preferable to encourage him to reform his ways. He was sent down to Bath so that he might help Mr and Mrs Ward, who managed the showroom, while the stock and accounts at Greek Street were checked, and was later given responsibility for reporting on the firm's Amsterdam agent. There, he found that

Above: *Creamware Nereid fruit centrepiece, circa 1870*

someone else had unknowingly been following his example, and having sold goods was making no attempt to pay for them. In October 1777 Mather again fell into evil ways and was said to have been spending his time drinking instead of doing his work. Again he was given a stern lecture in the hope of reforming him. Finally, in August 1780, after yet another effort to bring him to his senses, Mather's eleven years of employment, in which normal behaviour too often alternated with periods of disgrace, terminated in dismissal and he is no longer heard of. The partners could not have tried harder or been more patient with someone who so often rejected their compassionate gestures.

Group of pale blue and white jasper ornamental items; **Left:** *Bowl with additional yellow basketweave sprigging, circa 1785;* **Centre:** *Vase in form of bamboo tubes, circa 1800;* **Right:** *Ornamental bulb pot with bas-relief decoration of 'Sacrifice to Aesculapius', circa 1785*

Chapter Four

ETRURIA II

Wedgwood continued his work at Etruria experimenting with and perfecting new materials, in particular jasper, and collaborating with John Flaxman, George Stubbs and other artists in the production of plaques, cameos and other wares. In 1790 the Portland Vase, a reproduction in jasper of a 1st-century classical vase and the piece for which Wedgwood is perhaps most famous, was displayed to the public after several years spent on its design and manufacture. This put the final seal on Josiah Wedgwood's success, and before his death in 1795, he was able to make his three sons partners in his highly prosperous business.

Above: Solid blue and white jasper plaque featuring the 'Dancing Hours' with modelling attributed to Flaxman

The 'white biscuit' comprising Class III of the 1773 catalogue was the result of many experiments to perfect imitations of gems. As early as the middle of the 1760s Wedgwood had made trials with some clay from South Carolina sent to him by a friend in Manchester, precisely the same as some received by a local potter who said 'he could make nothing at all of it'.

The clay in question had been known in England since at least 1744. Wedgwood realised that the clay had possibilities, and began attempts to obtain a quantity of it for further experiments. He was very anxious to keep the matter as secret as possible, for fear of piracy by other plotters.

By chance, Wedgwood visited a friend whose brother had been recently in South Carolina, and who offered to return there in the role of agent to the potter. Details were settled and the man, Thomas Griffiths, set sail in the late summer for Charleston, Carolina, some 300 miles from the clay beds which lay in country belonging to the Cherokee Indians. Although Griffiths

obtained some clay and sent it back to Staffordshire, it did not serve the required purpose any more than some other American clay obtained from Pensacola, Florida.

Jasper

Research continued over the years, and by the middle of 1774 Wedgwood had got on the track of what promised to be success. He discovered that barium sulphate was the ingredient required, and with its aid was able to make a fine white stoneware that was ideal for his needs. The barium was obtained from Derbyshire, where it was known as 'cawk', and he was worried lest his secret should be discovered before he had reaped any benefit from it. Wedgwood stated that he dared not have it sent direct to Etruria, but suggested to Bentley that it might go to London and there be ground to a powder to disguise it prior to forwarding to Staffordshire.

Cameos

The new composition had a particular advantage in that it could be left white or coloured to choice. On New Year's Day 1775 in a letter to Bentley, after saying that he was glad the white body had met with approval in London and that he was confident he had mastered his production, Wedgwood continued:

*The blue body I am likewise **absolute** in of almost any shade, & have likewise a beautiful Sea Green, &*

several other colors, for grounds to Cameo's, Intaglio's &c. . . .

A fortnight later a further difficulty was reported after attempts had been made to fire cameos in one piece, when it was found that the background colour tended to stain the white relief. This defect was duly overcome; the plaques had their subjects affixed with a thin slip and were successfully fired complete.

Below: *Fireplace inset with Wedgwood jasper medallions*

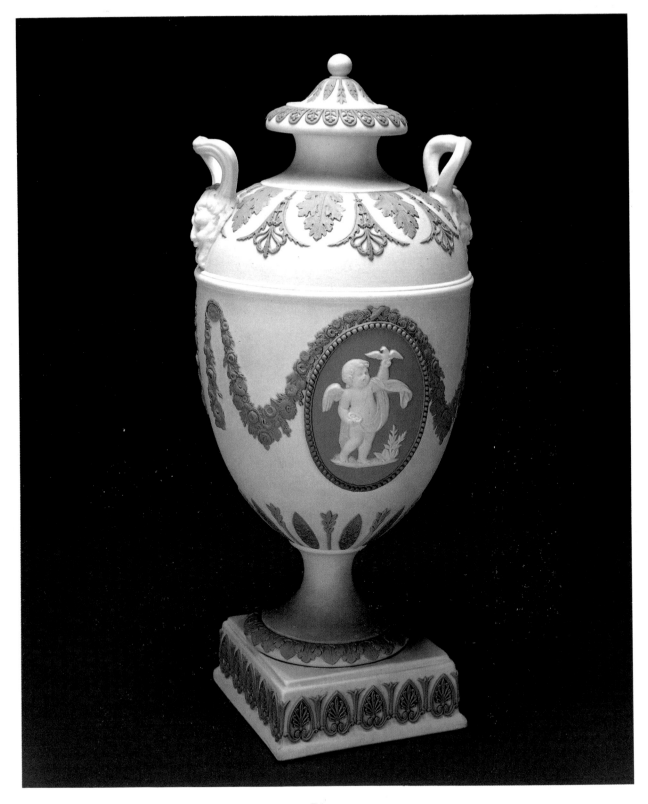

Above: *Wedgwood jasper cups and saucers, 1785–90*

In November 1775 Josiah Wedgwood referred to his new material for the first time by the name that has remained with it, 'Jasper'. He also said that he intended to make gems from it suitable for mounting as 'Bracelets Rings, &c.' However, not for a further two years was he fully satisfied, and it was only in November 1777, in a letter to Bentley, that he declared with confidence that he could make jasper with as much facility and certainty as black ware.

During the ensuing decades jasper cameos were made in their tens of thousands for a multiplicity of uses for which pottery had never before been employed. By 1779, many hundreds of different cameos and intaglios were in production, and there was a comparably wide range of portrait medallions of ancients and moderns. In addition there were plaques for insetting in snuff boxes and furniture; drums for the bases of candelabra and for opera glasses; buttons, beads and bell pulls; gems for chatelaines and watch keys; and not least in size and importance, tablets for chimneypieces and wall decoration. The new material proved to be even more versatile than had originally been hoped for.

Opposite: *Three-colour jasper urn-shaped vase with model of putto figure by Flaxman, circa 1780–90*

Jasper made a shy first appearance in the 1774 catalogue, where it formed class IV. In 1787, by when it had become established, the description was much less inhibited:

Below: *Black basalt figure by Giovanni Meli of Cupid Disarmed, circa 1880. Wedgwood Museum, Barlaston*

*IV. Jasper - a white porcelain bisqué of exquisite beauty and delicacy, possessing the general properties of the basaltes, together with that of receiving colours through its whole substance, in a manner which no other **body**, ancient or modern, has been known to do. This renders it peculiarly fit for cameos, portraits, and all subjects in bas relief, as the ground may be made of any colour throughout, without paint or enamel, and the raised figures of pure white.*

Jasper thus replaced the inferior 'waxen biscuit wear' of the 1779 catalogue. As regards colour, the pale cobalt to which Wedgwood's name is attached to this day, was the most popular, but the palette duly included dark blue, sage-green and brownish olive-green, lilac, yellow, and an intense black that differed from the basaltes.

A few years after the two-colour cameos went into regular production, continuing losses through discoloration during firing led in part to a further change. The jasper background had hitherto been coloured throughout the body, but spotting in addition to the high cost of cobalt led Wedgwood to introduce 'Jasper-dip'. For this, a white plaque was given a thin coating of coloured jasper on one or both sides, in the latter case making a sandwich of blue-white-blue that could be polished on the edges if required. Jasper-dip was produced from *c.* 1780, but solid jasper returned to favour and it is not possible to date examples solely from these indications.

John Flaxman and other artists

The quick success of jasper led to a need to increase the number of subjects for reproduction. In the selection of designers Wedgwood was at pains to employ the best artists available and whose style suited the medium. His most renowned modeller was John Flaxman, whose father, also named John, supplied Etruria with a number of plaster casts of reliefs and busts. The son, born in 1755, gained prizes for drawing at the age of eleven, and at fifteen attended the Royal Academy School. A bill of 1775 printed by Eliza Meteyard refers to the supply of bas reliefs of mythological characters, a set of 'The Seasons', and vases, signed 'for my father, John Flaxman, Junr.'

The younger Flaxman's work for Wedgwood in the years 1775-85 included portraits as well as tablets and a set of chessmen. In 1775 he was working on a likeness of Dr Daniel Solander, the Swedish botanist, and another of Joseph Banks (later, Sir Joseph and President of the Royal Society) his lifelong friend; both had sailed with Cook in the *Endeavour* and became nationally known. Flaxman also made bas relief portraits of the Duchess of Devonshire; Herschel, the astronomer; Charles James Fox; Captain Cook; William, son of Benjamin Franklin; Sarah Siddons; and John Philip Kemble. The larger compositions included the well-known 'Dancing Hours', 'Hercules in the Garden of the Hesperides', this at a cost of £23, and 'Apollo and the Nine Muses', of which four of the figures were modelled in 1775 and the others two years later.

Above: *Portrait of George III by studio of Allan Ramsay, circa 1767. National Portrait Gallery*

Among others who supplied material to Wedgwood in the 1770s for portrait plaques and other items were: Joachim Smith, who first achieved a name for himself when he presented George III in 1762 with a wax model of the infant Prince of Wales lying naked on a couch; John Bacon, later to achieve eminence as a sculptor; Theodore and Richard Parker, probably father and son, who

rendered accounts for casts of medallions and figures; Mary Landré, who was paid for plaster casts and '4 Boys in metal' at 7s. each; and two men better known as modellers of porcelain figures: Pierre Stephan, of Derby, and 'Tebo' (Thibault?) of Bow, Plymouth, Bristol and Worcester, neither of whom earned any praise from Wedgwood for their work.

Above: *Wedgwood jasper portrait cameo medallions, circa 1850;* **Left:** *Lady Walpole;* **Right:** *Duchess of Devonshire*

Opposite: *Two busts of black basalt, described by Wedgwood as 'equal in hardness to agate or porphyry'*

While he was so busy conducting the lengthy experiments that led to the triumph of jasper, Wedgwood was by no means free of other worries. One concerned Richard Champion, manager of the Bristol porcelain manufactory, which had been started in 1770 following the closure of Cookworthy's venture at Plymouth. William Cookworthy, an apothecary, had recognised in Cornwall the china stone that would combine with china clay to make a true hard porcelain of the Chinese or Meissen type, and had been granted a patent for his process in 1768. In 1773, Champion became owner of the Bristol works and two years later, when the seven-year life of the patent was due to expire, attempted to renew it for a further fourteen years.

Above: *Wedgwood jasper Cameos from collection at Clandon Park. National Trust*

miles south-east of Newcastle-under-Lyme. The argument against the monopoly was on several grounds, but in the main it was propounded that natural materials should not be restricted to any one user and so inhibit progress. In the end, a compromise allowed Champion use of the clay and stone in the manufacture of porcelain, but the Staffordshire potters were free to employ them for other products. The Bristol concern proved uneconomic and the patent was sold in 1781 to a company of Staffordshire potters who in turn, gained little benefit from it.

The bill relating to Champion's patent received royal assent on 26 May 1775, and on the 29th of that month Wedgwood, accompanied by John Turner and Thomas Griffiths, the latter having returned from America, set out for Cornwall. Josiah kept a journal in which he made notes of what he saw and did during the expedition, the purpose of which was, in his own words:

I thought it would be proper to take a journey into Cornwall, the only part of the kingdom in which they [the stone and clay] are at present found, and examine upon the spot into the circumstances attending them, — whether they were to be had in sufficuent quantities, — what hands they were in, — at what prices they might be raised, &c. &c.

The original patent specified that the use of the stone and clay should be limited exclusively to Cookworthy, then by purchase to Champion, and the extension was sought in the House of Commons. Wedgwood organised local support to oppose it; in particular he had the aid of John Turner, owner of a successful pottery at Lane End, a few

In due course the travellers reached Truro, the day before one of the periodical sales of locally mined tin, and ingots of the metal were displayed in the streets. Wedgwood had been warned to be on his guard when he was among the Cornish miners, who had a strong animosity towards Staffordshire potters in general and Josiah in particular, because their wares had displaced pewter at the table and so lowered the price of tin. However, the travellers encountered no difficulties and were able to arrange for supplies of what they sought at prices they were prepared to pay, leaving Thomas Griffiths at St Austell to supervise affairs on their behalf. By 16 June Wedgwood was back at Etruria where, after a brief rest, he was again hard at work pursuing his trials with the addition of the newly obtained materials.

George Stubbs

Two years later, Wedgwood became associated with the animal painter, George Stubbs, who had approached him for the provision of large plaques for his work. Stubbs had begun to experiment with enamel-painting and sought pottery as a possible base in place of the more usual copper. By May 1779 it would seem that Stubbs had received a fair number of usable plaques, so Wedgwood wrote to his partner about payment for them. The account was settled in kind, by paintings on pottery, a group portrait of the Wedgwood family in oils on a wood panel, and two models in relief for reproduction in basaltes or jasper: 'Phaeton and the Chariot of the Sun', and 'A Lion Preparing to Attack a Horse'. The pottery plaques were made of the 'white biscuit' modified to enable them to emerge from the kiln in suitably large sizes. It may be argued that Stubbs

Below: *Wedgwood pottery plaque by George Stubbs*

Above: Wedgwood jasper coffee cup and saucer. Castle Museum, Nottingham

used an idiosyncratic method of picture-making, but to have produced them was a remarkable achievement.

New ventures

Always aware of the vital importance of being one move ahead of the public, Wedgwood was sensing that buyers might be tiring of his Queensware and demand something new. In 1779 he introduced his 'Pearl White' to augment creamware, which had been marketed successfully for over a decade. As he wrote to Bentley in August of that year, he was perfectly satisfied himself with the well-tried favourite, 'but you know what Lady Dartmouth told us, that she and her friends were tired of creamcolor, and so they would of Angels if they were shewn for sale in every chandlers shop through the town'. The new ware was given some of its whiteness by the use of a glaze containing a trace of cobalt, which resulted in a perceptible blueness where the glaze gathered, such as round the foot-rims of plates.

It was at about the same date that Wedgwood was able to perfect a composition for the making of heat-resistant crucibles, and other articles for use by scientists and chemists. His life-long interest in the two subjects was shared with a number of men whom he met from time to time, or with whom he corresponded, including the clever and controversial Joseph Priestley whom he probably met through the Reverend William Willett, whose wife was Josiah's youngest sister. The range of apparatus produced at Etruria was gradually extended to include retorts, syphons, filter funnels and evaporating pans.

The correspondence between Wedgwood in Staffordshire and Bentley in London terminated abruptly in 1780, the last letter from the former being dated 12 November. A brief notice among the obituaries in the *Gentleman's Magazine* of that month announces the reason.

At Turnham-Green, Mr. Bentley, in partnership with Mr. Wedgwood. For his uncommon ingenuity, his fine taste in the arts, his amiable character in private life, and his ardent zeal for the prosperity of his country, he was justly admired; and will long be most sincerely lamented.

Bentley had moved in 1777 from his house in Greek Street to Turnham Green, where he lived near his friend, Ralph Griffiths. There is no record of the cause of Bentley's sudden passing at the age of fifty. He was twice married, his first wife dying in 1759 when giving birth to a child who died soon afterwards, and he married a second time in 1772, his widow surviving him. It is much to be regretted that no more than a very few of Bentley's letters to his partner have come to light. That they were retained and revered by their recipient is clear from a mention that Wedgwood kept them; according to his great-grand-daughter, Lady Farrer, he had them bound up in volumes known in the family as 'Josiah's Bible', on account of his having them so constantly by him. Without the letters being available today it is not possible to assess accurately the role of Bentley in the

Below: *Walnut and tulip wood commode, circa 1775, inlaid with Wedgwood jasper medallions*

Above: *Wedgwood's wife Sarah by Sir Joshua Reynolds*

The auction was conducted by Messrs. Christie & Ansell, predecessors of the present firm of Christie's, at their premises in Pall Mall, the sale beginning on 3 December and continuing for a further eleven days. A total of approximately £2,250 was realised by the 1,200 or so lots: an average of just under £2 a piece, which surely gave satisfaction to no-one except the buyers.

Each lot in the sale comprised a number of articles of similar type. A noticeable proportion of the lots went to 'S.N.' and 'N', both penned in a flowing script, leading to a supposition that these were perhaps *noms de vente*, either for Wedgwood himself or for one of Christie's staff acting on behalf of buyers wishing to remain anonymous.

Some of the purchasers were less reticent and can be identified. Among them was George, second Baron Vernon, who gave £1 15s. for a set of five basaltes vases ornamented with festoons, and Miss Fauquier, who became his second wife in 1786, who purchased busts of Demosthenes and Cicero for £2 12s. 6d., suggesting that she and her husband had in common a liking for the same make of pottery. Lady Pembroke, of Whitehall, paid no more than £1 5s. for two dozen cameos suitable for mounting as jewellery; but a few days later five Etruscan vases were bought by Sir Joseph Banks for £10 10s., a fair price under the circumstances. Undoubtedly many of the names are those of long-forgotten traders whom it is now difficult to identify.

To take Bentley's place in London, Wedgwood sent his nephew Thomas

partnership, but it is clear that Wedgwood relied on him as a confidant, and that he played a not unimportant part in the promotion of Etruria's products in England and far afield.

Following the death of Thomas Bentley, the stock of finished goods held jointly by the two men was disposed of by auction 'in concurrence with the wishes of Mrs. Bentley'.

Byerley, son of his widowed sister Margaret. Byerley had been a lively youngster and was an actor for some time before his uncle arranged in 1768 for him to go to Philadelphia. When Byerley returned to England in 1775 after having worked in New York as a teacher, he was given employment at Etruria, where his knowledge of the French language proved most useful.

The 1780s

One of Wedgwood's interests in the 1780s was the establishment of the General Chamber of Manufacturers of Great Britain, a body started to promote the interests of the country's manufacturers. Not least, it set out to discourage, if not prevent, the emigration of trained workers to foreign countries, whether on the mainland of Europe or America. This problem had come to Wedgwood's attention when some of his own men had left Etruria for employment overseas, and in 1783 he went so far as to write and print a pamphlet addressed to the remaining workforce, warning them of the perils that might overtake them if they joined their former colleagues. The Chamber played a part in 1785 in drafting a commercial treaty with the Irish, but this was abandoned following a lukewarm reception by both parliaments. More important to the potters were the treaties with France and Saxony, which resulted in a lowering of the high duties charged hitherto on English pottery sent across the Channel.

A few months prior to the signing of the French treaty in October 1787,

Above: *Josiah Wedgwood by Sir Joshua Reynolds*

Wedgwood sent his son John with Thomas Byerley to Paris, where they arranged for Dominique Daguerre to sell wares from Etruria. Daguerre, of the rue Saint-Honoré, was the foremost dealer in Paris, supplying furniture as well as expensive decorative objects to the Courts and nobility of many countries. He had obtained a near-monopoly in buying Sèvres porcelain tablets for mounting on furniture, and may have considered doing the same with jasper. However, when the cases of jasper and Queensware arrived from England he seems to have had most of them put in a cellar, made little or no effort to market the creamware, which formed the majority of the consignment, and the venture proved a failure. At the time of the Revolution Daguerre came to London, opening premises in Sloane Street where, among other clients, he numbered the Prince of Wales who had earlier patronised his Paris establishment. The Prince also gave his custom to Wedgwood, as among his numerous outstanding debts in 1795 for goods supplied earlier to Carlton House was the sum of £158 owing to 'Wedgwood & Co., of Greek Street'.

The 1780s also saw Josiah Wedgwood honoured by being elected a Fellow of the Royal Society, to which he contributed papers between 1782 and 1790. Some of these were on the subject of the pyrometer that he had devised for measuring the heat inside a furnace. Hitherto, reliance had to be placed on the experience of the fireman tending the kiln since the temperature reached was well above anything capable of being recorded by a mercury thermometer.

A welcome newcomer at Etruria was Alexander Chisholm, who had served as assistant to Dr William Lewis, chemist to the Society of Arts. Chisholm became a most useful employee, helping conduct the endless experiments, performing general secretarial duties for Josiah, and helping to educate the children. As the years passed he increasingly acted as private secretary, many of Wedgwood's later letters and notebooks being in Chisholm's handwriting.

Widening the range

The range of goods was further widened by the making of vases and other ornamental pieces in jasper ornamented with bas reliefs. Among them were vases and covers for decoration, vases for flowers, candle-sticks, and teawares of such elegant design that they could only have been intended for display in cabinets. A modeller, Henry Webber, son of a Swiss sculptor, Abraham Wäber, was taken on the staff in 1785, and proved an excellent craftsman: he had been recommended by Sir Joshua Reynolds 'as the most promising pupil in the Royal Academy'. Another Academy pupil, John Lochee, executed portrait-medallions from *c.* 1774, and a few well-connected amateur designers were able to have their work accepted, notably Lady Templetown, Lady Diana Beauclerk and Miss Crewe.

A further series of bills from John Flaxman reprinted by Eliza Meteyard list some of the work on which he was engaged between 1781 and 1787. Figures, busts, a tureen, portraits, plaques commemorating the French treaty, and a set of chessmen show how varied were his commissions. The portraits included one of Dr Samuel Johnson, from an

Opposite: *Solid blue and white Wedgwood jasper Venus or snake-handled vase, circa 1787*

engraving thought to have been one made by Thomas Trotter from his own drawing.

In the autumn of 1787 Flaxman set out for Rome, Wedgwood advancing him money for the purpose, the artist's objective being to forward his studies while providing drawings and models for the factory. He was joined there for a time by Henry Webber, and also secured the services of a French sculptor, John Devaere, who later came to work at Etruria. Several Italian artists were also recruited by Flaxman, so there was an ample supply of fresh material flowing back to Staffordshire.

Also received at Etruria was a consignment of clay from Australia. This was sent in 1789 by Governor Philip on the instructions of Sir Joseph Banks and Wedgwood pronounced it to be excellent.

The Portland vase

Some years earlier, in 1778, Wedgwood had sent as a gift to Sir William Hamilton at Naples a jasper tablet of 'The Apotheosis of Homer'. A few years later Hamilton became closely involved in the events surrounding the article that was to be the finest and most famed of Wedgwood's productions, and one that provided a triumphant climax to his career as a potter: the object eventually known universally as the 'Portland Vase'. The original vase was made in the late first century A.D., of dark blue glass overlaid with opaque white glass, possibly in Alexandria but generally referred to as of 'Roman' origin. According to tradition it was excavated from a tomb in Rome in the year 1582, and received its first mention in print sixty years later when it was described as one of the treasures of the Barberini palace.

By the early 1780s, when the then owner of the Barberini palace sold it, allegedly because she had contracted large debts from gambling, most connoisseurs and students were aware of its existence. The buyer was a Scot, James Byres, who sold it to Sir William Hamilton who, in 1783, brought it to England and sold it to the Duchess of Portland, a notable collector of all kinds of curiosities. When the Duchess died eighteen months later, her collection was sold by auction and the vase bought by her son, the third Duke of Portland.

Wedgwood had known of the vase from engravings and had been eager to reproduce it in jasper, so he must have been particularly elated when he signed a brief document on 10 June 1786.

I do hereby acknowledge to have borrowed and received from His Grace the Duke of Portland the vase described in the 4155th lot of the Catalogue of the Portland Museum . . . and I do hereby promise to deliver back the said Vase . . . in safety into the hand of his Grace upon demand.

Detailed drawings of the vase were completed within a year, principally by Henry Webber. It was only after these

Opposite: *The 'Portland Vase', Wedgwood's most celebrated masterpiece*

Above: *Detail from the base of the 'Portland Vase'. About 30 of these vases were made*

further long years of patient trial and error that it became possible for Wedgwood to arrange the public showing of an example at Greek Street, at the aptly named Portland House, during the months of April and May 1790. This was accompanied by a document declaring the vase to be 'a correct and faithful imitation, both in regard to the general effect, and the most minute detail of the parts' signed by the President of the Royal Academy, Sir Joshua Reynolds.

As soon as it could be spared from Greek Street the vase was placed in the hands of Wedgwood's second son, also named Josiah, and Thomas Byerley, who set off with it on a tour of Europe. They visited The Hague, Amsterdam, Hanover, Berlin and Frankfurt where they showed the vase, and other Etruria productions, to heads of state, the nobility and anyone else of importance who might be interested.

It is thought that about thirty of the vases were made successfully during Josiah's lifetime, but of these some remain untraced. Among the latter is the example taken round Europe, which has been said erroneously to be in the British Museum. In subsequent years the firm made many thousands of copies of the Portland Vase (in the late 1830s with the figures demurely draped), but the 'first edition' is probably the finest, and certainly the most celebrated, of Etruria's wares.

The last years

In 1790 Josiah reached the age of sixty, and on 16 January of that year he made his three sons, John, Josiah and Tom, and Thomas Byerley partners in the business. The firm was styled Josiah Wedgwood, Sons and Byerley but at the time John and Tom had little or no desire to become potters. As a result, in June 1793 the firm became for a time Wedgwood & Son & Byerley. During these years old Josiah was in semi-retirement, taking holidays at Buxton,

Below: *Queensware triangular jelly mould and cover, circa 1790. Jelly was poured into the plain outer mould, with the decorated section inverted in it. After unmoulding, the painting was revealed through a coating of jelly*

Blackpool and the Lakes, and making a tour in Wales. An idea of his scale of living at Etruria Hall is provided in a list made in May 1794: there were seven male servants from butler down to gardener. In addition ten horses were kept, two four-wheeled carriages and one two-wheeled.

On 3 January 1795, in his sixty-fifth year, Josiah died. He was buried in the porchway of the parish church of St Peter, Stoke-on-Trent, and when the church was rebuilt in 1829 his remains were removed to the churchyard. A monument to him was placed in the chancel in 1803, and this was duly re-sited in a similar position in the new building; the monument taking the form of a shaped slab of black marble on which is an inscribed tablet of white marble supporting a Portland vase and a basaltes ewer. Above the tablet, carry-ing the inscription composed by Sir James Mackintosh who combined the callings of philosopher and judge (in the vice-admirality court at Bombay) and was a brother-in-law of John and Josiah II, is a head of Josiah Wedgwood by John Flaxman.

Wedgwood left a considerable sum of money, including £30,000 to each of his sons, £25,000 to each of his daughters, and the Etruria estate with the Hall and

Above: *Jasper vase, circa 1780, designed by Flaxman for Wedgwood*

Opposite: *Pair of solid blue and white jasper figure candlesticks, circa 1785, depicting Ceres* (left) *and Cybele* (right)

manufactory to Josiah. It was a remark-able termination to the career of a man whom Jewitt informed his readers started in life with 'the poor and miserably small sum of twenty pounds'. What Jewitt conveniently omitted to mention was the fact that Josiah's wife brought him the money with which Etruria was built, and that he doubtless received help, if not also legacies, from, his numerous relatives. Be that as it may, it is beyond argument that, in the formal words on his monument, Josiah Wedgwood 'converted a rude and in-considerable manufactory into an ele-gant art and an important part of national commerce' - and so it remains.

Wedgwood lustreware bowl, circa 1920, decorated with butterflies

Chapter Five

FROM 1795

Sadly, none of Josiah's sons shared their father's enthusiasm for the business, which soon went into decline. The trend towards mass production resulting from the Industrial Revolution left its mark on Wedgwood wares, with inevitable lowering of standards in design and finish, and an overall deterioration in quality. However, the firm again enjoyed a revival as from the 1870s, with some especially memorable commissioned work in the 1930s, and has continued to be productive right up to the present day, the premises having moved to Barlaston in 1940. The Wedgwood Museum there has done much to promote the image of the firm.

When Josiah died the partners remaining in the business were his son Josiah II and Thomas Byerley, the latter in charge at Greek Street. There, the twenty-one-year lease was on the point of expiry and a move was made to another location, this time to Westminster, to a house at the east corner of St James's Square and the present Duke of York Street.

Of old Josiah's three sons, two had married the sisters Elizabeth and Louisa Jane Allen of Cresselly, Pembrokeshire, and Tom, the youngest, remained a bachelor. None showed more than a fraction of the deep interest their father had had in Etruria, and as all of them were wealthy they had no compelling reason to do so. After splitting from his brothers in 1793, John in 1800 rejoined the firm, remaining a partner for twelve years, but giving it only occasional if keen attention. Then he found to his alarm that much had deteriorated over the years; Byerley had done his best to keep things going, but he was not a practical potter and lacked authority.

Nevertheless, there were a few innovations, among them the so-called 'pastry-ware': unglazed caneware tureens resembling pies that would hold cooked meat and could be brought to the table. They had been suggested as early as 1786, but nothing seems to have come of the idea for a decade, when their sudden popularity was due to a shortage of wheat flour at the time.

Copper, silver and gold lustres were also marketed. They had been known of at Etruria before 1795, but were only perfected and used there at later dates. They were principally employed on creamware, the 'Moonlight' lustre,

Above: *Caneware teapot and milk jug, circa 1860. Wedgwood caneware was produced from circa 1775*

comprising gold and various colours applied in the form of marbling, being much admired. On pearlware, a pink lustre was used with good effect.

In order to increase production and keep the manufactory up to date, the creamware department was enlarged and a steam engine installed. This was made and erected by Boulton and Watt during 1801 at a cost of £1,095, improvements being made to it seven years later.

By 1804 John had moved from Bristol to Seabridge, from where he could exercise closer supervision. In February 1804 he wrote to Josiah, in Dorset, reporting on some of the confusion he had found, and a year later could offer little further encouragement: he told how the creamware 'has lost its softness and evenness of surface, which constitutes its great beauty', because it was being fired in the same kiln as pearlware. The latter required a higher temperature than the cream, so he proposed the obvious solution of firing the white on its own. A couple of months later, in April 1805, John was

Below: Game pie .dish, circa 1820, an example of Wedgwood pastry ware

Above: *Wedgwood plate with willow pattern decoration, introduced by Thomas Minton in the early 1790s. Victoria and Albert Museum*

less anxious, and at the end of the year the firm began marketing tablewares printed with patterns in underglaze blue, a type of pottery that many of their neighbours and competitors had been making and selling in increasing quantity for a number of years. It was made in direct competition with the 'Nankin' imported from China, so the earlier patterns were of Oriental inspiration; typical of them was the 'Willow-pattern', introduced by Thomas Minton in the early 1790s and subsequently widely imitated. Etruria entered this particular market with a design referred to at the time as 'Bamboo'.

Then came a series of floral patterns, some in blue but others in brown, most likely due to John Wedgwood's great interest in botany and horticulture, which had led to the founding of what is now the Royal Horticultural Society.

One of the brown-printed patterns was the 'Water Lily', decorated in underglaze brown, the first use of this colour in printing, embellished with

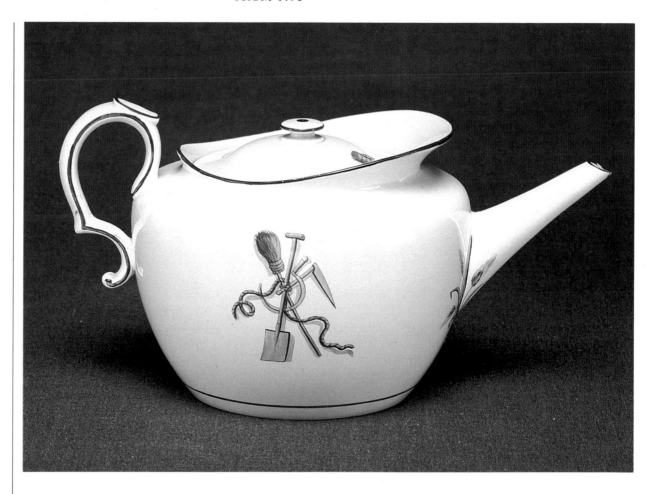

Above: *Creamware parapet-shape teapot, circa 1805, decorated with print and enamel 'Agricultural Implements' pattern*

touches of orange and gilding to give a rich effect.

In addition to entering the market with their new blue-printed ware, Etruria continued to produce the old favourites: basaltes, jasper, creamware and so forth. Byerley, then in London, was urging John and Josiah to send him greater quantities of articles and to introduce some new ones.

In the summer of 1807 Byerley crossed to Dublin, and bought a large house in the city which he converted into a showroom, and which it was hoped might attract the people, or their sons and daughters, who had patronised

Josiah Wedgwood nearly forty years earlier. Etruria was informed of how the new rooms were to be set out with a different type of ware in each, 'but I should feel more secure if we had something *peculiar*, and in this respect the Jasper may still befriend us, for there is very little of it in the market'. Byerley added, 'what we have of it is, I fear, however, more calculated to stand

on our shelves and be admired than to produce profit.'

Despite the recurrent complaint that nothing new was coming from Etruria, there was at least one attempt to meet a likely demand. The government declared that 25 October 1809 should be a public holiday, Jubilee Day, George III having been proclaimed King on 25 October 1760 and now entering into the fiftieth year of his reign. To commemorate the event, the firm made some suitable inscribed articles, of which a bulb pot is illustrated. The decoration is printed in no fewer than three colours: orange-red, purple and brown, with the oriental flowers hand-painted in colour.

Thomas Byerley died at the end of 1810, aged sixty-two. He had spent over thirty years with the Wedgwoods, father and sons, and without doubt could not have helped comparing the exciting times of the elder Josiah with what ensued after 1795.

Porcelain

In 1812 came a completely new introduction, something never attempted before by a Wedgwood: porcelain. The formula used was similar to that employed by other English makers of the time; a quantity of calcined bone being added to china clay, china stone and flints to produce the material known as 'bone-china', that remains to

Above: *White biscuit half-jug, circa 1820, used as a traveller's sample. Wedgwood Museum, Barlaston*

Opposite: *Wedgwood brown stoneware jug, circa 1840, distinguished by its hand-applied enamel decoration*

this day an esteemed British product. But as Wolf Mankowitz has indicated, old Josiah would have launched the new product very differently. The half-hearted way in which it was introduced to the public shows 'very clearly the limitations of the factory in the years which followed his death'.

Wedgwood bone-china continued to

be sold until as late as 1829, but production of it may have ceased at an earlier date with orders being filled from stock. It would seem to have been most in demand about 1815-16, when the Marchioness of Lansdowne ordered some bowls decorated with a pattern of 'hawthorn buds and leaves, varied by red and green lines', and a member of the Rothschild family purchased a dinner service decorated with 'blue and gold diamonds, surrounded by blue triangles, edges of the articles in gold'. Both painting and printing were used to decorate china with oriental, floral and other subjects, but it would seem that Wedgwood's traditional restrained styles were unable to compete with their rivals' florid patterns.

In 1819 experiments took place for the making of a 'stone china', which was marketed in the year following. It was a dense and opaque ware, described by the late Tom Lyth of Barlaston, as being similar in appearance to French hard-paste porcelain but greyish in tone. Each piece was given a printed mark, together with a pattern number which allays any doubts as to what it is. Decoration invariably took the form of printed outlines filled-in with hand-painted colours and gilding. Manufacture ceased by 1861.

Above: *Wedgwood dish in the form of a leaf. Smithsonian Institution, Washington DC*

Opposite: *Wedgwood jasper pot pourri vase and cover, circa 1851*

For one reason and another trade had declined so much that it was decided in 1828 to dispose of the London showroom, selling both the premises and the stock. From the summer of that year a clearance sale took place, not only the ornamental and table wares but also the moulds and trial pieces that had accumulated. The firm retreated to Staffordshire without the benefit and prestige of a London outlet of its own.

In the years following 1812, when John Wedgwood relinquished his interest in Etruria, changes continued to occur. In 1823 Josiah II's eldest son, Josiah III, became a partner but failed to take an active role in the pottery. Josiah's third son, Francis, was made a partner in 1827 and settled down to the arduous task of reactivating the concern. In the year after the death of Josiah II, which occurred in 1843, the entire Etruria estate, the pottery, village, Hall and all else, was offered for sale by

auction, but the manufactory did not change hands. In the middle of 1843 Francis took into partnership John Boyle, who died only eighteen months later, and was followed from 1846 to 1859 by Robert Brown. Three of Francis's sons successively became partners, and members of later generations of the family followed suit, so that today the name of Wedgwood is still to be found among the directors of the company.

The mass-production resulting from the Industrial Revolution and its use of

Above: *Wedgwood white majolica salad bowl with spoon and fork, decorated with coloured transparent glaze, circa 1880*

Opposite: *Black basalt teapot, circa 1840–50, enamelled with flowers*

steam-power inevitably led to a lowering of the quality of design and finish. The reaction to this began to appear during the early 1840s, when the long-somnolent Society of Arts, Manufactures and Commerce (later, the Royal

Society of Arts) initiated a series of annual exhibitions. Prizes were awarded for the best items in each class of goods.

During the same decade Henry Cole established Felix Summerly's Art Manufactures, bringing together designers and makers to produce articles that met Summerly's criteria. Those participating included Wedgwood among whose contributions was a salt-cellar in the form of a dolphin supporting a shell on its back, made of pearlware, coloured and gilt, the marks including Felix Summerly's initials and the name of the designer, John Bell, in full. Another was a set comprising a shaving-pot, and brush-handle depicting 'Heroes

Overleaf (left): *Wedgwood earthenware slip-painted vase, circa 1880*

Overleaf (right): *Rare earthenware inlaid and enamelled vase, lid and stand by Thomas Mellor, circa 1880. Wedgwood Museum, Barlaston*

Bearded and Beardless', designed by Richard Redgrave, and shown at the 1848 Society of Arts exhibition. Redgrave is known also to have designed a porter cup for the Wedgwood Summerly venture.

The Great Exhibition

Wedgwood's also played its part in the Great Exhibition of 1851. The exhibition was divided into sections of classes according to the goods displayed; class 25 comprising 'China, Porcelain. Earthenware, &c.', shown in the North Transept Gallery of the great iron and glass 'crystal palace'. The firm's display embraced all their current productions, and from the number and variety of the articles in the catalogue it is clear that they made a big effort to regain some of their lost importance.

The jury judging class 25, under the chairmanship of the Duke of Argyll, reported that the articles shown by the firm 'are of great as well as long-acknowledged merit — which consists chiefly in a faithful revival of forms originated by the elder Wedgwood, some of the most remarkable of which were suggested by the genius of Flaxman', and Wedgwood's were awarded a Prize medal.

At the head of the list of the firm's exhibits was their new 'Carrara' ware, which had been produced from 1848 to meet the public demand for white marble-like statuettes, named after the famous quarries at Carrara, in Tuscany. In later years, more figures, groups and busts were added to the number shown in 1851.

Eighteenth-century Wedgwood basaltes and jasper were already being sought by collectors, and a selection of specimens was loaned to the important Art Treasures Exhibition, held at Manchester in 1857. Five years later, at a comparable showing of national treasures, this time at the South Kensington Museum, London, a much larger selection of old Wedgwood was displayed.

Interest in the old undoubtedly stimulates interest in the new: in this instance, in modern copies of period Wedgwood. However, the firm could not live completely in the past, and had to do its best to compete with its contemporaries. One of these was Mintons of Stoke-on-Trent, who displayed examples of their recently perfected 'majolica' at the 1851 exhibition. This ware bore no resemblance to the similarly named 15th- and 16th-century Italian *maiolica*; the latter was a coarse buff pottery coated with an opaque white glaze that could be painted in colours, whereas the Victorian was a white pottery decorated with coloured transparent glazes.

The principal exponent of majolica at Etruria was Emile Lessore. He fled from France in 1858, and after a few months with Mintons transferred to their rivals. Lessore had a highly individual style, quite dissimilar to that of the average china-painter, which is more akin to the miniaturists; his slight yet assured draughtsmanship often recalls some of the pen and ink sketches of the Tiepolos, especially in the depiction of *putti*. He invariably signed his work.

Emile Lessore remained at Etruria

until 1863, when he decided that he could no longer resist returning to his native land. There, he continued to decorate Wedgwood ware, which was sent across the Channel to him and was duly returned to Staffordshire.

Various fashions in printed ware came and went over the years. The middle shade of blue was replaced by a ghostly pale blue, which was rivalled in popularity by brown, green, raspberry red and others. Then, in the middle of the 1830s came a liking for a blurred dark blue, named 'flowing blue' or 'flow blue', achieved by the use of a 'volatilising agent' in the kiln causing the printed lines to spread and flow in the glaze. It was still being made in the 1870s.

Other types of ware that had a fashion in their day include those made in imitation of Saint Porchaire or Henri II pottery. This, too, was following in the

Below: free hand-enamelled horse's head on creamware, by Colonel Henry Hope Crealock, whose animal paintings featured on Wedgwood ware circa 1874–7

Above: Boat Race Goblet, designed by Eric Ravilious for Wedgwood, 1938, as part of a revival of black overglaze printing

footsteps of Mintons, where their employee Charles Toft made close copies of the original pieces. The cream or white clay object was decorated by having a pattern impressed in the soft surface, the cavities being filled with stained clays of which the surplus was removed. Wedgwood's made a chess table in the style that, it was said, was for use with John Flaxman's chessmen: they must have formed a remarkable combination. Another novelty was the use of photography in decoration.

Memorials to Wedgwood

Local pride in their most distinguished citizen led in 1859 to the forming of a committee to supervise the erection of a statue to commemorate Josiah Wedgwood, the statue to be paid for by public subscription. The sculptor chosen was Edward Davis and Wedgwood was represented with a Portland Vase in his hand, cast in bronze. The statue still stands where it was first unveiled on 24 February 1863, in front of Stoke-on-Trent railway station.

Another project to the same end was also slowly coming to fruition: a Wedgwood Memorial Institute to be sited in Burslem. The idea of this had preceded the intention to have a statue, but being a much larger scheme it required greater and more sustained effort. Eight months after the formalities at Stoke the first stone of the Wedgwood Institute was laid, the ceremony being performed on 26 October 1863 by one of the most popular figures of the day, the Rt. Hon. W.E. Gladstone. It was an indication of the regard in which Wedgwood was still held that no less a political figure than the Chancellor of the Exchequer should travel from London for the occasion, and that he should follow the brief stone-laying by a speech of considerable length.

In 1865 two books on Wedgwood appeared, by Llewellynn Jewitt and

Eliza Meteyard. Jewitt rushed to get his published first, but he had been unable to gain access to the vitally important documents owned by Joseph Mayer and had to manage without them; the result was in the nature of *Hamlet* without the prince. The documents had been promised to Miss Meteyard, who made good use of them.

After so many decades in decline or merely static, the Wedgwood company began to recover some of the enterprise they had enjoyed in the days of old Josiah. Charles Toft left Mintons for Etruria to become chief modeller (1872-89). From the same factory in 1876 came Thomas Allen, who became chief designer and art director at Etruria until he retired at the age of seventy-four in 1905. Allen's signed works included a striking series of pseudo-Elizabethan characters from Shakespeare printed in pottery plaques.

The firm initiated two important

Below: *Terracotta cup designed by Keith Murray for Wedgwood, 1935*

changes: in 1875 a London showroom was again acquired, and three years later the making of bone-china recommenced to continue uninterruptedly to the present day. The showroom at Holborn Circus was at first shared with a manufacturer of medical glassware who also represented Wedgwood's. Ten years later, the latter had the place to themselves, and in 1890 a move was made to 108 Hatton Garden. In 1911 a further removal took place to 26-7 Hatton Garden, where the firm remained until the early 1940s.

The Wedgwood Museum

In 1906 a Wedgwood Museum was opened at Etruria, sufficient interesting and historic documents and pottery having been assembled despite the loss of so much at the dispersal of the contents of the York Street premises in 1828-9. A catalogue was compiled by the London dealer and Wedgwood specialist, Frederick Rathbone, who provided brief descriptions of the 448 exhibits as well as introductions to the various types of ware on display and a chapter on the marks used by Josiah and his successors.

Although there was a steady flow of new shapes and decorative patterns, Wedgwood's continued to rely largely on the reissue of old and loved patterns. These were brought up to date by the alteration of such details as handles and knobs, suited to the taste of the time.

A new member was added to the design staff in 1912, Daisy Makeig-Jones, who in due course initiated a series of wares that broke completely with the Wedgwood tradition with regard to shapes, patterns and colours. She created a strange world inhabited by imaginary folk copied from the works of Edmund Dulac and other book-illustrators, using fairies and goblins, dragons, butterflies and much else. They were printed in gold outline on vividly coloured lustred grounds on bone-china, the vases and other objects being in shapes reminiscent of those of 18th-century Chinese porcelain. Nothing could possibly have been more distant from the neo-classical simplicity of Josiah's day, but the British public of the 1920s liked and bought it.

At the close of the decade, Wedgwood's countered the world-wide recession by attempting some innovations. They followed their founder's formula by commissioning work from leading artists and modellers, including John Skeaping, Eric Ravilious and Keith Murray. The first-named modelled a series of highly stylised animals; Ravilious engraved some interesting patterns for a revival of black overglaze printing; and Keith Murray designed some shapes that would have earned the approval of the first Josiah.

In addition to the difficult trading conditions then prevailing, another problem urgently demanded attention: Etruria was proving inadequate for modern manufacturing methods and could not be enlarged as other premises had been erected in its proximity. Also, the building was slowly and steadily subsiding. It was decided that a move should be made to Barlaston, five miles distant to the south-east, where a new

factory and village would be built. This duly took place, the first part of the new building being opened in 1940, with the remainder gradually taking shape and being fully occupied ten years later. Etruria, which had been in use for a total of 181 years, was left standing ghost-like and empty, being finally demolished in 1966.

Since moving into their new premises, Wedgwood's have continued making the wares for which they have for so long been famous, continually adding to them as is essential in a competitive world. Among the products that have become increasingly popular are articles suitably inscribed in commemoration of some old or new, public or

Above: Pair of inlaid earthenware pillar candlesticks and teapot circa 1870. Wedgwood Museum, Barlaston

private, occasion. This is no more than a continuation of old Josiah Wedgwood's 'First Day Vases', his 'Prince of Wales Vase' or his Bastille medallion and other pieces referring to events in his lifetime. A similar continuity is exemplified in the present-day making of wares in 18th-century patterns, employing for the purpose moulds from the original blocks. There could be no better tribute than this to the far-seeing man who started it all.

China lidded vase with Fairyland Lustre design 'Ghostly Wood'. Designed by Daisy Makeig-Jones circa 1920. Wedgwood Museum, Barlaston

114

Chapter Six

COLLECTING WEDGWOOD

Wedgwood wares are highly collectable, and the collector's task is made a lot easier because most of the specimens are clearly marked. (A selection of the most common Wedgwood marks are shown at the end of this chapter.) Josiah Wedgwood realised early on the importance of marking his products – especially when imitations of his wares began to appear. Many of these early forgeries still exist, and can sometimes be very deceptive. As early as 1759 he began to put his name on his products, and from 1769, the year when Etruria was opened, products were stamped with the names of the partners, Wedgwood and Bentley.

The Wedgwood collector is considerably aided by the fact that most genuine specimens are unequivocally recognisable. Early in his career Josiah Wedgwood realised that to mark his products in a particular way would gain the public's confidence and help to establish his reputation. As early as 1759 Wedgwood began to put his name to his wares, and from 1769, the year when Etruria was opened, the productions of that manufactory were stamped with the names of the partners. The fact that the marks were impressed into the clay body by means of a metal stamp meant that they were difficult to remove, the use of acid or a grindstone for the purpose leaving a tell-tale depression. The effectiveness of Wedgwood's marks can be gauged by the existence of

Above: *Wedgwood jasper ware heart-shaped trinket box*

imitations that appeared in his lifetime, causing him much anxiety.

The simple word 'Wedgwood' was used continuously from the start. From 1891 it was given the addition of ENGLAND, and then MADE IN ENGLAND, which obviously helps in dating, but to distinguish between basaltes and jasper made in the 18th century and that of the Victorian era requires experience. It is best to look upon a mark on any kind of chinaware as no more than a confirmation of other signs, and to consider these with care. It may be of assistance if the characteristics of the best pieces are considered.

For basaltes, jasper and other 'dry bodies' such as caneware and rosso antico they are as follows:

The most obvious sign is the high quality of finish, with every detail rendered clearly even when a relief is on a small scale. In successive decades the sharpness is likely to have diminished. Where a portion of a relief stands out it would have been undercut; work that was executed by hand much more painstakingly in the 18th century than at later dates.

The old pottery bodies were freed from impurities so far as was possible, and finished plaques and vases have much smoother surfaces than later specimens. To the finger an old piece has been described as having a 'wax-like' feel, 'which has the resistance of velvet without being woolly', whereas later ones are quite different to the touch and the white reliefs have a dry chalky appearance. Creamware is likewise distinguishable as regards old and new: the earliest, which is seldom marked, is a rich, almost buff, colour and is thickly glazed.

Eighteenth-century marked pieces are noticeably light in the hand, the glaze is thin and evenly spread and the general finish neat. Later examples are heavier in weight, piece for piece, often thicker and less carefully finished. It is sometimes easy to overlook an impressed mark on a piece of glazed creamware, as the glaze may have run into the stamped letters.

More than one writer has averred that old Josiah Wedgwood used to appear in the factory from time to time inspecting the goods being made. If something did not come up to his

Overleaf (left): *Wedgwood black basalt oil lamp supported by slaves, circa 1780*

Overleaf (right): *Wedgwood black basalt vase*

Right: *Wedgwood teapoy*

Above: Bone china coffee pot, coffee can and saucer with Coronation pattern. Designed by Stan Wedgwood 1936 for the Coronation of Edward VIII. Wedgwood Museum, Barlaston

standard, it was said, he would smash it with his walking stick or throw it on the floor saying: 'This is not good enough for Josiah.' Whether there is truth or not in the story is beside the point, but it has led to the supposition that everything that left Etruria was absolutely perfect in every particular. However, there is evidence of the opposite having taken place, and that Wedgwood was a realistic businessman who did not tolerate waste of goods that might be sold.

In 1769, in a letter to the London showroom, he mentioned creamware 'seconds', of which an increasing quantity was accumulating at Etruria. Wedgwood suggested that they might be disposed of in London, as they 'will never sell here at all, nor go along with the 2nd Table service we make up for Liverpool'. This is a clear indication that inferior ware was sent across the sea regularly.

Forgeries of Wedgwood wares exist and can sometimes be very deceptive, many of them being as old as their originals and bearing the characteristic signs of age. The Sèvres factory made some good versions of jasper plaques in the late 19th century, but the majority of Continental-made 'jasper' is of more recent date and is likely to deceive only beginners. It differs from Wedgwood in being poorly finished and, above all, in having been moulded in one piece, relief and all, with the background colour applied by brush round the outlines of the raised portion.

The more dangerous of the copies are those that were made in Staffordshire at the time when Wedgwood was making the prototypes, in particular, the copies of seals made by John Voyez, a modeller who worked for a short time at Etruria and then went to prison for an unspecified crime. The work of Voyez is hard to detect, but his contemporaries were less daring in their piracies, putting their own, or no, name to their work. Among the marks used was one employed on seals which looks at a glance as if it is authentic, but closer inspection reveals that the name in minute lettering is WADGWOJD.

Creamware was no less extensively copied than the other Wedgwood productions. It was made at a number of English factories, notably at Leeds, Liverpool and Swansea where, in each case, marks were only used occasionally. Across the Channel a number of French factories competed with English importations, in some instances employing Staffordshire potters to assist them. Other factories were active in the Netherlands, Germany, Scandinavia, Hungary, Italy, Spain and Russia.

Below: *Wedgwood Queensware;* **Left:** *Victorian covered kitchen jug, circa 1850;* ***Right:*** *teapot, circa 1780, transfer-printed to commemorate the death of General Wolfe*

WEDGWOOD MARKS

Wedgwood — Probably the first mark. Supposed to have been used by Josiah Wedgwood at Burslem 1759–1769.

WEDCWOOD — This is a very rare mark, used at the Bell Works 1764–1769.

WEDGWOOD
Wedgwood — Used in varying sizes from 1759–1769.

 The circular stamp, without the inner and outer rings, and without the word Etruria is doubtless the earliest form of the Wedgwood and Bentley stamp, 1769.

 This mark, with the word Etruria, was fixed in the corner, inside the plinth of old basalt vases. It is sometimes found on the pedestal of a bust or large figure. 1769–1780.

 This circular stamp, with an inner and outer line, was always placed around the screw of the basalt, granite and Etruscan vases, but is never found on Jasper vases. 1769–1780.

Unique script mark, Wedgwood & Bentley, 1769–1780. — *Wedgwood & Bentley*

Mark used on Wedgwood & Bentley intaglios, with the catalogue number varying in size, 1769–1780. — Wedgwood & Bentley 356

Very small intaglios were sometimes marked W&B with the catalogue number, or simply with the number only, 1769–1780. — W. & B.

Rare mark found only on chocolate and white seal intaglios, usually portraits made of two layers of clay with the edges polished for mounting, 1769–1780. —

These marks, varying in size are found upon busts, granite and basalt vases, figures, plaques, medallions and cameos, from the largest tablet to the smallest cameo, 1769–1780. — WEDGWOOD & BENTLEY / Wedgwood & Bentley

Varying in size, these marks are attributed to the period after Bentley's death (1780) and probably used for a time after Josiah's death (1795). — WEDGWOOD / Wedgwood / WEDGWOOD / WEDGWOOD

WEDGWOOD & SONS

Very rare mark used for a short period in 1790.

JOSIAH
WEDGWOOD
Feb. 2nd 1805

Mark of Josiah Wedgwood II. Supposedly a new partnership or change in the firm. Found only on some basalt tripod incense burners. It may be the date when the design was first registered, 1805. Sometimes '2nd Feby' appears instead of 'Feb. 2'.

WEDGWOOD

The mark upon the bone china or porcelain, made 1812–1822, always printed either in red, blue or in gold.

WEDGWOOD
WEDGWOOD

From 1769 to the present day this mark has been impressed in the clay on Queen's Ware, or printed in colour. In recent times the words Etruria and Barlaston and the name of the pattern have in many cases been printed in addition to the trade mark. From 1780, ornamental Jasper, Black Basalt, cane, terra cotta and Queen's Ware are always marked with this stamp. The name 'England' was added in 1891.

WEDGWOOD
ETRURIA
WEDGWOOD
ETRURIA
Wedgwood
Etruria

These marks are rarely found on pieces of a very high character. Adopted about 1840 but used for only a short period.

This mark, now in use on bone china, was adopted in 1878 when the manufacture of bone china was revived. It is printed in various colours.

England was added to the mark Wedgwood in 1891 to comply with the American Customs Regulation known as the McKinley Tariff Act.

ENGLAND

Mark used today on bone china, developed from mark of 1878.

This mark, printed in colour, is being used today on Queen's Ware, starting in 1940.

INDEX

ACKNOWLEDGEMENTS

The publishers would like to thank the following for their kind permission to reproduce photographs in this book: Bridgeman Art Library 13, 14, 60, 65, 74, 75, 79, 83, 93, 94, 96, 97, 100, 104, 105, 106, 121; Victoria & Albert Museum 110, 111; Christie's 67; Michael Holford 98, 116; National Portrait Gallery 55, 77; National Trust Photographic Library 19, 38, 41, 118; Octopus Group Picture Library/M. Holford 31; City Museum and Art Gallery, Stoke-on-Trent 37, 102; Castle Museum, Nottingham 52, 82; Wedgwood Museum 73; National Trust 80, 119; Smithsonian Institution 103; Spectrum Colour Library 15, 117; Victoria & Albert Museum, By Courtesy of the Board of Trustees of the, 12, 90; Sotheby's 11, 24; City Museum, Stoke-on-Trent 8, 21; Wedgwood Museum, Barlaston, Staffordshire, England, Courtesy of the Trustees of, cover, 2, 4, 6, 10, 16, 17, 22, 23, 26, 27, 28, 29, 32, 33, 34, 35, 36, 42, 43, 44, 46, 47, 48, 50, 51, 54, 57, 58, 59, 61, 63, 64, 66, 69, 70, 72, 76, 78, 81, 84, 85, 87, 89, 91, 92, 99, 101, 107, 109, 113, 114, 120.

The publishers would also like to thank Mrs Lynn Miller, Information Officer at the Wedgwood Museum, for her patient help and cooperation in submitting photographic material.